Flying Tiger
A Crew Chief's Story

The War Diary of a Flying Tiger American Volunteer Group Crew Chief with the 3rd Pursuit Squadron

Frank S. and Terry M. Losonsky

Schiffer Military/Aviation History
Atglen, PA

Acknowledgements

A special thanks to the team who helped put the book together: to Gale McAllister (crew chief) and his wife Ruth who let us share a special moment in his life (see February 9, 1942), Frank Andersen (crew chief), Morgan Vaux (communications), Don Rodewald (armorer), Ken Jernstedt (pilot), Keith Christensen (armorer), Roland Richardson (communications), Carl Quick (crew chief), Dan Hoyle (administration), and many other AVGers who graciously gave their time.

Thanks also to R.T. Smith (AVG pilot), Bill Minkel (crew chief), Phil (Army pilot) and Chris Losonsky (Navy pilot), Paul Hamersley, Gary Coker (pilot), all aviation enthusiasts, who reviewed our drafts. We gratefully appreciate the time Pat Revis, Wanda Ter Keurst, Richard Stewart, Dawn Stolzfus, Ken Olthoff, and Ruth Monagin spent proofing the manuscript.

And a very special thanks to our wives Nancy and Joyce who have seen us through thick and thin. Our families, Terry, Phillip, and Chris. Terry's family, Andrea, Natasha, Nicole, and Ryan.

Book Design by Ian Robertson.

Printed in China.
ISBN: 0-7643-0045-8

We are interested in hearing from authors with book ideas on related topics.

Published by Schiffer Publishing Ltd.
77 Lower Valley Road
Atglen, PA 19310
Please write for a free catalog.
This book may be purchased from the publisher.
Please include $2.95 postage.
Try your bookstore first.

Contents

Introduction

Much of the "Flying Tiger" history was written from the pilot's viewpoint. Those brave pilots deserve much praise, but those of us who fixed the "ships" and kept them flying also have a history. Although our story is perhaps not as flashy, we believe it is quite interesting and in tune with the everyday spirit of that intense time.

This book was written with help of my war diary, over 200 personal photographs, and the help of many friends. Terry and I tried to capture the spirit of the time by combining diary entries and photographs, supplemented with interviews and dialogue. We believe this format provides the reader with a multi-dimensional view of the period.

The book will give aviation historians new insight into the days shortly before the Flying Tiger successes in late 1941.

THE TIME LINE: JUNE 1939—THE PRESENT

The Time Line represents the significant events described in this book.
Beet Fields Michigan, 1938-1939
Enlisted in the U.S. Army, Aug 2, 1939
Attended Chicago Aeronautical University—Engine and Prop School Nov 1939—March 1940
AVG Adair Recruitment at Selfridge Field Michigan, May 1941
Transferred to West Palm Beach June—July, 1941
Board the "Jaegersfontein" July 7, 1941
Arrive Honolulu July 15, 1941
Arrive Rangoon Burma Aug 15, 1941
Training—Toungoo Burma Aug 16, 1941
"Dry Season—Burma" Oct 10, 1941
Defense of Rangoon Burma Dec 12, 1941
Retreat to Toungoo/Lashio Dec 28, 1941

Retreat to Kunming Dec 29, 1941
P-40 Salvage Job Wenshan March 7, 1942
Paoshan Bomb Transport April 17, 1942
Rainy Season May 1, 1942
Gale McAllister's Retreat May 10, 1942
AVG Disbanded July 4, 1942
South Africa Aug—Nov 1942
Arrived Miami Nov 27, 1942
Hired by CNAC, a subsidiary of Pan American, as a senior mechanic in 1943
Hindustan Aircraft Company as a senior mechanic—1944
Ford Motor Company building B24s
AAF cadet—1945
Aircraft maintenance supervisor at Clark Field, Philippines
Import-export business in Manila, and joined Philippines Airlines
Line maintenance supervisor Philippine Airlines—1947
Chief of Maintenance and pilot Trans Asiatic Airlines (TAA)—1947-1950
Farming—1950
Senior jet engine service engineer, Allison Division of General Motors—1951-1981
Executive Officer and Board Member of Part IV, A Columbus, GA, Restaurant Group-1978

THE EXCHANGE RATES 1941-1942

In 1941/42 the following exchange rates were in effect: $2.00 Singapore = $1.00 U.S. dollar; $50 Chinese = $1 U.S. dollar; 3.50 Rupees (Burma) = $1.00 U.S. dollar. Some prices in the diary are in the form: 8/3/8 rupees. The expression translates to 8 rupees /3 anna /8 pice.

AREA MAP 1941-1942

The map identifies significant locations referenced
in this book.

Chapter I
The Adventure Begins

October 8, 1920—August 2, 1939

I was born October 8, 1920, in Detroit, Michigan, to immigrant Czechoslovakian parents. My mother died when I was five, and my father remarried a year later to Klemenetina Besko. Times were slow and hard for my father's barber business, so my stepmother worked hard for low wages in a factory making metal springs. I remember her coming home with hands cut so bad that they bled. Afterwards, she would cook and clean the house. I really liked her. With the crash of 1929, times went from bad to worse. I stole coal from coal cars to keep our house and business heated. I also shined shoes and delivered morning newspapers with my sister Ann. We supplemented the family income with home brew and moonshine—quite illegal of course.

I was educated by the Catholic nuns at St. Cyril's in Detroit, Michigan. They paddled me for eating lunch in Church—not a pleasant memory. In the ninth grade I moved to my aunt's farm near Ashley, Michigan. I walked 2 1/2 miles to and from school each day and twice a day during baseball and basketball season. I left my aunt a year later and struck out on my own. I lived with any family who would take me in; paying them $5.00 or $6.00 a week for room and board. I lived with the Barnes's, the Bachman's, and the Martis's. I worked hard milking cows, working the peppermint and beet fields, and even doing a stint as a soda jerk at the local drug store. In my senior year I quit school but couldn't find a job so returned and graduated in June of 1939. My sister and I were

close during these times. She sent me $5.00 every so often, and in my senior year gave me a '35 Essex. The county garage supplied used oil to keep it going.

August 2, 1939
I enlisted in the Army Air Corps August 2, 1939

On August 2, I signed on with the Army Air Corps and was sent to Selfridge Field, Michigan. The Air Corps offered independence, a steady job, and a future in aviation. My entry test scores were high but not high enough for flight school (I failed the physics section).

March 1941
The Air Corps sent me to school, then back to Selfridge Field to work on the new P-40s.

In March, the Air Corps sent me to study new aircraft engines at the Chicago Aeronautical University. After I graduated I went to Chanute Field, Illinois to study propellers. I studied hard, made good grades, and thoroughly enjoyed the technical schools. After the technical schools I returned to Selfridge Field, Michigan, and worked on a variety of new engine types like the new P-40 C15 Allison engine.

April—May 1941
Skip Adair visits Selfridge to recruit volunteers to help the Chinese Air Force.

Enlisted in the Army Air Corps.

Working on the new P-40s.

In 1939, the Japanese launched an all out air war to defeat the Chinese by bombing every major city in free China. The Japanese air force was virtually unopposed. On April 15, 1941, President Roosevelt signed an unpublished executive order establishing the American Volunteer Group (AVG). The purpose of the executive order was to stop the Japanese invasion of China and keep the Burma Road open. The Burma Road was China's lifeline to the outside world.

The executive order stated that U.S. officers and enlisted personnel could join the AVG without penalty. The volunteers would remain U.S. citizens, and

The new P-40s at Selfridge Field, Michigan.

after the one year contract expired they could return to their service without loss of rank. But in spite of the protection offered by the executive order we AVGers were not recognized as full members of the armed services nor afforded true veteran status until years after the war, but that's another story.

Claire Chennault, a long time China veteran, was chosen to head the new group. The AVG was considered a covert operation and the Central Aircraft Manufacturing Company (CAMCO) was selected to serve as the organization's front. CAMCO's president, William Pawley, was authorized by the U.S. government to hire a cadre of personnel including one hundred pilots and several hundred ground personnel, medical staff, radio personnel, armorers, and assorted administrative personnel.

In May, Skip Adair, one of Chennault's recruiters, came to Selfridge and talked to a group of us about joining an elite organization going to China to support the Chinese people. Adair was looking for folks with P-40 experience to support the small Chinese Air Force. Pay was good. Mechanics were offered $350 per month, (four times what the service paid) food, medical, housing and transportation allowances. I immediately filled out the forms. My First Sergeant, I believe it was Sgt. Hayes, had to sign for me because I was under 21.

The CAMCO contract basically states that: (1) "The Employer operates an aircraft manufacturing, operating and repair business in China"; (2) "That Employer agrees to employ Employee to render such services and perform such duties as the Employer may direct"; (3) "The term of the contract is one year"; (4) And "in the event of the total disability or death of the Employee suffered in line of duty, the Employer, upon receipt of such proof of such total disability or death, shall immediately pay to Employee, or to the Employee's designated beneficiary as the case may be, a sum equal to six months' salary."

At the time I signed, I wasn't motivated to save the world, or run away from anything. Nor was I unhappy with the Air Corps. The reason were the money, a subsidized trip to the Orient, and the promise of adventure. A sidebar; pilots were paid $600, flight leaders $675, and squadron leaders $750. Although never stated in the pilot's contract, pilots were to receive a $500 bonus from the Chinese government for every Japanese plane shot down.

One or two of our guys almost missed the AVG experience. Frank (Jake) Andersen was fixing aircraft controls when Adair handed out applications. If it hadn't been for Frankie Satella's mother, Jake may have missed the boat. Frankie's mother refused to give her son permission to join the AVG (Frankie was under 21) so Frankie gave Jake his application. Jake recalls using lots of "white-out" before he could fill out the application and send it to Adair.

In March President Roosevelt signed the Lend-Lease Bill, Hitler issued a directive for the invasion of the Soviet Union, and the Blitz on London continued with two major attacks on the 16 and 17 of April.

June, 1941
The squadron transferred to Morrison Field, West Palm Beach for training.

Several weeks after the Adair visit, my squadron left for West Palm Beach, Florida. As Frank Andersen recalls, "We left Selfridge Field in Frank's (Losonsky) hot convertible, two buck sergeants, less then a year in service, without a care in the world. The first night we stopped at a CCC camp in Kentucky. The Camp Commander, a young lieutenant, came out and greeted us. We gave him a snappy salute which thrilled him to death. Eventually we got to Morrison Field, West Palm Beach. Rumors had it we might go to the Philippines. Most of us young folks were excited. The Philippines sounded romantic and exotic, but the "old timers" told us we were crazy. They'd been there and insisted it was primitive. They told us that we young folks had no idea what we were getting into. 'You don't want to go to the Far East—no way.'

Eventually the Army did send some of the guys from Morrison and Selfridge Fields to the Philippines. Quite a story: The Selfridge Field squadron had a number of married men called "shack men." The "shack men" lived in town and every morning reported for duty. At night they returned home. Shortly before we entered the war, the Army decided to transfer some of them to the Philippines. The "shack men" threatened to desert so the Army backed a train up to Selfridge field, loaded them on board and shipped them to San Francisco, under armed guard. After the Japanese invaded the Philippines some of the men ended up in the Battan Death March. I've lost track—I don't know how many survived, but if Frank and I hadn't volunteered for the AVG we may have easily been one of them."

In West Palm Beach, I soon forgot the China thing and went about getting my student pilot license. My instructor, Dot Lemon, soloed me in 6 1/2 hours for $50 (June 21, 1941).

June 30, 1941
Selected as the youngest "Flying Tiger" Crew Chief.

I believe it was mid-June when Adair notified several of us that we had been selected for China assignment. He said the service would discharge us at "government convenience." CAMCO would hire us and

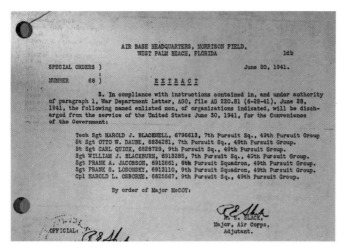

AVG (or Air Corps) Orders.

we were to report aboard a passenger liner in San Francisco called the Jaegersfontein by 7 July. CAMCO would pick up all travel expenses.

Two days later I was discharged, re-hired, and processed for a passport. The passport listed me as a student. I was the youngest of the 48 AVG crew chiefs.

I left West Palm July 2, spent the 4th in Ashley, Michigan, with my future wife Nancy. The next day I visited my sister in Ionia, Michigan. On the 6th, I took a train to Detroit and from Detroit flew to San Francisco on a TWA "sleeper." The goodbyes were much too fast.

On 2 July the Japanese held an "Imperial Conference." They made a decision that Japan should take

Goodbyes—Suzanne (Nancy's sister), Myself, Nancy (my future wife), Mabel (Nancy's mother), and Aunt Mary.

Indochina even at risk of war. The U.S. had broken the Japanese diplomatic code and knew about the event. On June 22 the Germans attacked the Soviet Union under the code name "Barbarossa."On July 4, President Roosevelt broadcasts: "The United States will never survive as a happy and fertile oasis of liberty surrounded by a cruel desert of dictatorship."

July 7, 1941
Went aboard the ship. Got a state room with Jake (Andersen) and Blackburn. Bought a 45 automatic for $32.00. Got a $25.00 advance. The ship is very nice and a swell bunch of fellows. Don't know when we will set sail.

This was my first time aboard a passenger liner. The accommodations were luxurious. I don't recall being nervous. Just a feeling of great adventure.

A side shot of the ship.

I sold the pistol in China for $750.00, almost two month's pay. Not a bad investment.

The DC-5s were stored in the cargo hold behind me.

July 8, 1941
Boat still hasn't sailed. Had coffee served at 11:00 am, a Dutch custom. Breakfast was very good, but at dinner, I never ate a meal with so many changes of plates. Had tea at 4:00 pm, another Dutch custom. Had supper at 7:00 pm, quite fancy. Pay started July 6, 1941 at $11.62 per day. They loaded two DC-5s on the ship. Also cars—Studebakers. Went to Chinatown. Got back on board at 1:10 pm. Rumors are we sail tomorrow.

"Dining" was an adventure, all-be-it a bit intimidating. Dutch cuisine was fascinating, especially the "foreign food." As a 20 year old who had just come from the sugar beet fields, it took the greater part of the ocean voyage to figure out which fork to use, when and where. What an education!

The pay was great. I went from $84.00 to $350.00 a month. I banked most of it—I wanted to buy a farm (I did, in 1950—80 acres near Ashley, Michigan).

Someone once told me Douglas built fifteen DC-5s. Amazing—we had two of the fifteen on board.

I thought Chinatown was going to give us a "taste" of the real China. Boy, was I in for a surprise. Chinatown, San Francisco, USA was nothing like the real China.

July 9, 1941
Still boarding the ship with cars and fruit. The weather is hazy and cool. The last bunch of fellows are coming on board. There will be 140 of us CAMCO men. CAMCO had bought $700.00 worth of musical instruments, records. We learned that two young nurses came aboard today and they will sail with us. We have a makeshift swimming pool on board. Makes me think of West Palm Beach. Jake, Carl Quick, Otto Daube and I went out one last time. Bought some liquor. We got aboard at 1:30 pm quite high.

It turned out we sailed with 123 CAMCO employees, not the 140 I noted in the diary. I kept an informal status of the folks in the margin of my passenger list.

Boredom, drinking, and gambling were very much a part of the early American Volunteer Group (AVG) experience.

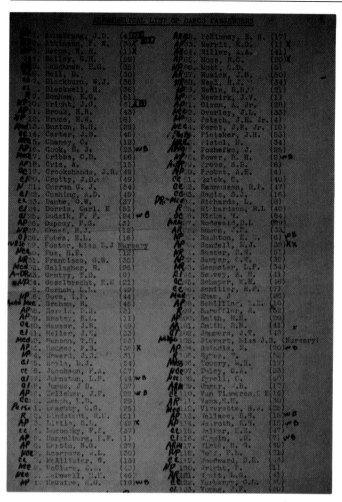

The CAMCO passenger list.

"Red" Foster.

The two nurses were Red Foster and Josephine Stewart. Both girls were pleasant and great conversationalists.

July 10, 1941
This morning I was introduced to Mocha, a kind of coffee, in the social room. At our morning meeting we were told no one was to leave the ship. Everyone is eager to start...The passes were taken away and the signed passports were all set now. At 1:20 pm we were off. Everyone seems happy. At 3:30 pm we lost sight of the Golden Gate bridge. At 8:30 pm the ship was blacked out for our protection. I played cards and won $40.00.

Although the U.S. was not at war with Japan, we were still worried about Japanese submarines. I believe had the Japanese sunk us, the U.S. may have entered the war 6 months earlier at a cost significantly less than half the Pacific fleet. I also believe the Japanese saved their "silver bullets" for the bombing of Pearl Harbor and coming invasion of the Pacific rim. Fortunately the AVG groups reached Burma safely via three different ships. The U.S. would remain neutral for another five months.

Poker was a popular card game enjoyed by most, and played every day I was at sea. Some of the boys made lots of money.

July 11, 1941
Lost 1/2 hour overnight (You lose "time" traveling West). Didn't sleep much. Sea was very rough. There are a few of the fellows quite sick. We have lifeboat drill at 1:00 pm. Captain says we will be in Honolulu Monday am. Won $130.00 shooting craps. Lost $35.00 at Blackjack.

Life vest.

I was never seasick but plenty of my friends were. Seasickness lasted a few miserable days. The boys would hang over the rail and barf—sad sight. I felt sorry for them. I don't believe the Doc or the nurses gave them anything—they just had to gut it out.

As I recall we had a couple of drills. The drills lasted about a half hour. I put on a life vest, reported to my lifeboat station and waited for the all clear.

July 12, 1941
Lost another 1/2 hour. The weather is nice and warm, but the sun still hasn't shone. We have all kinds of games. At 9:30 pm we finished with our program. It was a quiz on songs. As part of the games, we had sing-alongs. A few of us would get up and sing some of the popular tunes, like "By the Silvery Moon."

We didn't discuss what we would be doing or where we were going. I don't believe we had any technical material available. Our shipboard "programs" were strictly civilian. I had no assigned duties. What a lark, I'm having a terrific time on this passenger liner, no work, eating like a king and I'm getting paid for it!

July 13, 1941
Went to Sunday services held by the Captain. Played two games of shuffleboard. The Captain promises the pool will be open when we leave Hawaii. Sea is getting rough this PM.

A Javanese crewman.

The Captain's Sunday service consisted of Bible reading and singing.

The Dutch Captain was a pleasant sort of chap. The crew was mostly Javanese and didn't speak English so I had little contact with them.

July 14, 1941
They opened the swimming pool, but only three feet of water. Listened to a lecture by Dr. Pan on China. It was OK. The evening's perfect. The stars are out.

The Doctor was returning to his homeland, I don't recall if he was with the AVG. He talked about Chinese customs, and the plight of the people under Japanese oppression.

The Jaegersfontein swimming pool. Swimming was a welcomed diversion.

July 15, 1941
Sighted Moliki about 1:30 pm. We arrived Honolulu 9:30 am. Went ashore, bought a few post cards. It sure is a rugged town, all sailors and soldiers. The town isn't very clean.

Mt. Pilo.

Sightseeing in Honolulu.

Honolulu was on war footing. Soldiers and sailors were everywhere.

July 16, 1941
Took a trip around the island. Saw many interesting things. Took many pictures. I went to Mt. Pilo, which

Hawaii departure.

was most interesting. Got back to the ship just before it sailed at 1 pm. Threw the lei away just as tradition says. I hope it gets back to shore. We are on our way to Manila.

Tradition has it that if a lei returns to shore you will return to Hawaii. My lei must have reached shore because Nancy and I returned to Hawaii in 1970 on the way to my last overseas assignment in the Philippines.

I believe the ship's purser told us we were going to Manila, Philippines. Eventually we docked in Rangoon Burma, but at the time we had no idea where we were going.

July 17, 1941

Went for a swim. At 8:30 we were stopped by two U.S. cruisers, the Salt Lake and Northhampton. We were held up until 10:30 until two signal men came aboard. We followed the two cruisers by about 1/4 mile. I hope we convoy with them all the way to Manila. Took a few pictures of the ships. It's getting hot and muggy. We have to keep our portholes closed. No lights.

It was reassuring to have the Navy escort. We thought we were "valued cargo." Ironic, later the Navy refused to have much to do with us. I quote from the Chief of Navy Personnel 31 August, 1945.

"AVG service is not counted as active duty for promotion or length of service for those who reenlisted in the Navy, or Marine Corps...Since AVG service is not active service in the Armed Forces of the United States, personnel will not be entitled to receive or wear the honorable service lapel button on basis of AVG service alone."
Signed R.H. Hillenkoetter, Captain USN

It took years before the government recognized the AVG as a U.S. fighting unit, supporting U.S. National interests.

The cruiser "Salt Lake."

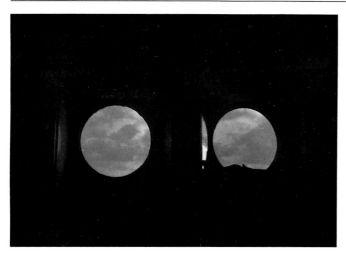

Ship's "air conditioning."

The air inside the ship was often hot and stale. The ventilation system consisted of forced air through small cabin vents. If the portholes were closed, the ventilation stopped. The crew closed the portholes during stormy weather and blackouts.

Sunning.

July 18, 1941
Another swim, and sunbathing, followed by tea, a vaccination, and a cholera shot.

July 19, 1941
Another swim, sunbathing, then to the barber who develops my film for .50 cents a roll. The photographs are turning out good, so far. Ran into a rain storm, looks bad, the ship's beginning to roll. Won a game of Monopoly.

I had a small Brownie camera and shot a couple of rolls of film going over.

July 20, 1941
We're going to cross the equator tomorrow and the crew's getting a party together. The "shellbacks" who are the seasoned sailors are brewing up an initiation for the rest of the fellows who haven't been across the equator. It's very hot now. We are somewhere near the Howland Islands.

July 21, 1941
We were "polliwogs" until 10:00 am. Then we crossed the equator. The initiation was quite rugged. They painted us, ducked us in the pool, fed us fish, then made us official shellbacks. All had a good time. We have been going south since we left Hawaii.

They made us eat raw fish, then they greased our bodies with some ungodly concoction of dough mixed

Nurses.

with cod liver oil and milk. It took three days to wash the stuff off. As part of the show the nurses pretended to "flash" us—quite spectacular.

July 22, 1941
Got up at 3:00 am and went out on the deck to sleep. It's hot. Even the pool water is hot. At 4:30 pm our course changed to west about 45 degrees. The rumor is that we are going to Australia. Hope so.

Australia sounded exciting. Almost as exciting as China. Maybe a little less dangerous, lots of beer, and English speaking girls.

I grabbed a blanket and spread it on the deck. No mattress, no sheet, no pillow.

July 23, 1941
Didn't sleep well, the deck was too hard. But it is feeling a little cooler. Took my typhoid shot today. Bought a Topi, it's a Javanese sword, also a Djouge, it's a Javanese boy with his fighting rooster.

I hated those shots. I was plenty anxious before getting them. Must be why I wrote so much about them in the diary. Other AVGers had similar experiences. Morgan Vaux recalls, "Not long after I arrived in Yunnanyi, a Chinese female nurse gave me a cholera booster shot. The needle was very dull and I believe she sterilized it in a container of what looked like 'saki' wine."

July 24, 1941
Another sleepless night. I think we crossed the international date line, but they won't tell us anything. Our direction is N.W.W. Last night was tough. That typhoid shot really made my arm stiff. There isn't much to do except sit out in the sun and burn. I'm black as a Negro now. We are limited on fresh water and are running low on it.

Baths were taken in the swimming pool—no soap. I don't recall if we used deodorants.

July 25, 1941
It's raining, so had a cool night's rest. Got my second cholera shot. I sure feel down today. It's still raining.

July 26, 1941
We crossed the International Date Line. So this date is left out. Get this straight. Today is Friday, tomorrow is Sunday. We are getting good reception on the ship's radio from some nearby island.

Radio was enjoyed by all. It kept us in contact with the "outside." They piped the radio over the ships' loudspeakers.

The US and Britain freeze Japanese assets. Roosevelt orders the Philippine Army merged with the U.S. Army. MacArthur is given command of the forces. On July 30th, Japan bombs the U.S. gunboat "Tutiula" in Chungking. Japan apologizes.

July 27, 1941
About all there is to do outside is sweat and swim in the salt water pool. The pool gives you a heck-of-a sore throat if you swallow any of it. It's going to be good to see land again and walk on it. This tub's been rolling like a rocking chair for two days now.

July 28, 1941
Still no land, we ran into storms, the last at 4:30 pm, not bad though. It's been hazy all day. Didn't do much today. Swam a little and played Monopoly. It passes the time. The fastest is about two hours a game. Jake and I were talking about West Palm Beach today. Boy how these memories do hurt. Lost a buck playing Black Jack.

Monopoly was popular because it was new and based on high finance. The average game took 2 to 3 hours so took up slack time between meals, shots, and sleep.

July 29, 1941
Got up at 4:30 am. My throat was sore and couldn't sleep. Missed out on sick call so bought a bottle of Listerine and gargled it. It gave some relief. Today makes 14 days without seeing land. Believe it will take us 6 to 8 more.

July 30, 1941
Went to see the Doc about the sore throat. He said it was influenza, nothing serious. At 4:30 the Northhampton sent off two of its scout planes and they were gone for over an hour. We are headed S.S.W. Am reading "What's A Heaven For." It isn't a very good book.

July 31, 1941
Perfect weather. Isn't much to do except wait until we get to Manila. It's 4:30 pm now and we get our shots at 5:00. Typhoid and Cholera.

August 1, 1941
Beginning of the month found us at sea for 21 days. The Captain said that we would be in Rangoon by the 18th of August. I hope so, my arm was sore last night, but much better today.

Roosevelt stops all shipments of oil and aviation fuel to Japan.

August 2, 1941
Shuffleboard tournament. Jake and I are partners. We start playing Monday. 11:00 am, we were picked up by a heavy Dutch cruiser. The U.S. cruisers left

Taking on the pilot.

us going West. We must be near the Dutch East Indies. 8:00 pm We have stopped. No black out tonight. We are anchored between some islands. We took on a British pilot. He will take over tomorrow.

August 3, 1941
We got underway at daybreak. We passed lots of small islands and coral reefs. I believe that's why we took the pilot on. No one knows where we are. There seems to be no life on the islands. Rumor is that we

"Gun Island"—Tories Straight.

are approaching the Tories Straights. 1:30 pm we let the pilot off. We were told that all film would be taken and destroyed. The ones we took showed up big guns mounted along one end of the island, also a scuttled ship. My legs are tired for some reason, I'm gaining weight and it's getting hot again.

August 4, 1941
Got tight last night on champagne. Cost $45.00 a bottle. Had a vicious hangover this morning. Played our first game of shuffleboard tournament. We lost 79 to 69. At 5:30 pm we passed an oil tanker, the "Bastista." The moon is about full. What a night. The ship's purser demanded all cameras be turned in. He also wanted any pictures of the U.S. cruisers, the Dutch cruisers, and the island with the guns.

As I recall I took a number of pictures of the cruisers, and several of the island but I refused to give up the film or the camera.

August 5, 1941
Today was one of those days you just don't know what to do with yourself. Lost our second game of shuffleboard. Saw a few of the big islands off to the West just before dark. Won $15.00 playing blackjack. Moon's full, its 9:45 pm and it's muggy. We must be getting close to the equator. Direction is N.W.W.

August 6, 1941
Won a shuffleboard game today. Weather is hot. Got our "shellback" seals. Slipped down and almost broke my leg. I did bruise my rump. At 6:30 saw two islands about 4,000 feet high. Direction N.W.W. We should steer due North tomorrow.

August 7, 1941
Won another shuffleboard game. Makes us .500. Got our last typhoid shot today. Arm is stiff. We passed a large island at 7:30. I saw campfires on the island. The island is about 9,000 feet high, so high I couldn't see the top. We should be turning North if we are headed to Manila. If we don't I guess Java is our next stop.

We had crude maps and the help of several Navy people who were able to approximate our location. One Navy chap even fashioned a crude sextant that worked!

August 8, 1941
Was sick today from the typhoid shot. Arm is sore, and I'm sleepy. We stopped by some island. Some cruiser was getting fuel. We stayed from 7 am until 1:30 pm. It sure is hot. Lost at shuffleboard, but won $45.00 at blackjack. Jake owes me $10.00. Parker owes me $5.00. We are going full speed now, direction N.W.

August 9, 1941
The Captain posted a bulletin. We dock in Singapore Monday morning. Already have my stuff packed.

What a surprise. We thought we were going to Java, Australia, or the Philippines.
Roosevelt and Churchill meet in Newfoundland. If British or Dutch possessions in the Far East are attacked, they agreed that it is understood that the U.S. will enter the war.

August 10, 1941
Everyone is sweating the port. All are packing and getting ready to leave. I'm in a $60.00 pool. We had a good dinner last night, two kinds of wines. We also got some nice souvenirs, a teak wood stamp box. I bought some Dutch stamps and coins.

I was collecting stamps and coins as a hobby. I didn't collect to sell.

August 11, 1941
We landed today, went ashore at 1:30 pm. This sure is some town, dirty and hot. The money is 2:1 ($2 Singapore dollars = $1 U.S. dollar) here. I bought a pith helmet, shorts and long socks. Rode in the rickshaws all day. Those coolies sure do work hard. The town is mostly Hindu. Ate dinner at the YMCA with an English couple. What a brogue. CAMCO has no plans for us Tuesday. Lots of mixed people in Singapore.

Those coolies worked hard but I wasn't sorry for them. They seemed a happy lot, and most important, they had a job. Jobs were important to those of us who had gone through the depression.

Rickshaw riding.

August 12, 1941
The works are screwed up. We can't leave the ship because we are scheduled to sail for Rangoon at 2 pm. They had to put the baggage back on the ship. Bought a bathrobe, 4 polo shirts, a pair of sandals, silk handkerchiefs, cheap, from the boat vendors. We expect Rangoon in 3 1/2 days. We are not being convoyed. Bought all kinds of coins before I left. It is hot!

What a show. The boat vendors came up alongside the ship. We would point to what we wanted. The vendors threw the items up and we would toss the money down. Sometimes the money landed in the water. No problem, the vendors' helpers would jump into the water and get it.

August 13, 1941
Slept most of the day. The sea is calm. Expect to be in Rangoon Saturday morning. We are in the Bay of Bengal. It is hot and muggy.

August 14, 1941
It's rough. Nothing to do but sleep. Its even too hot to do that. Jake and I were talking about West Palm Beach and all the girls we went with. Nancy has been on my mind all day. She was the one I really was in love with and I still think I am.

August 15, 1941
Entered Rangoon and proceeded up the river about 5 miles. We won't go ashore until tomorrow.

The Irrawaddy was black and muddy and not the type of water I wanted to fish or bathe in. The natives, on the other hand, didn't mind doing either.

The native women were quite stunning but shy.

Chapter II
Burma The Training:
August 16-December 7, 1941

August 16, 1941

Left the Jaegersfontein at 8 am. Had lunch at the "Silver Grill" in Rangoon. Left Rangoon for Toungoo at 11:00 AM on a French narrow (10) gauge railroad. On the way we passed rice fields and water buffalo. Our first stop was Dabein at 11:45. Second stop Pegu at 12:25. Quite a large place. Got a quart of beer for 50 cents. Had lunch at Pyuntaza 1:40. Hodges threw money at the Hindus. They did everything but kill themselves. Mailed Ann and Nancy letters. Arrived at Toungoo late in the pm. Toungoo is about two miles from Kyedaw, our air base. We live in grass huts, wooden beds, with straw mattresses and pillows. We are really in the jungle. It is hot. We have three P-40 Tomahawks. The rest are to be ferried from Rangoon. Our contract year with CAMCO begins today.

Airfield entrance.

The airfield from the tower.

The base was laid out north—south with a large airstrip running down the middle.

Our ready shack was a grass hut on poles. I don't recall any phone hook-ups in the hut. The pilot's ready shack was much better but both places were hot as blazes in the summer.

View of the camp.

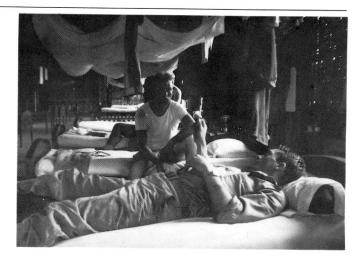

Sleeping quarters.

The Kyedaw ready shack.

Our thatched barracks.

The pilot's ready room.

The toilet and washroom.

The grass/thatched huts, wooden beds, straw mattresses and pillows were, despite the appearance, quite comfortable.

The Burmese toilet was a cement floor with two holes in the ground. Had to be careful, a miss was a mess for Aumba our toilet man. He always carried a small wicker broom and a 2 qt. can. He visited the toilets every day and put them in perfect shape. He was a proud chap and skilled at his toilet cleaning trade. Morgan Vaux recalls "The latrine at my radio station was a large deep hole with a plank across the middle, surrounded by low walls. The unsanitary conditions bred rats, yet no cats were ever seen." I don't believe Morgan had an 'Aumba' to clean his toilet.

Make no mistake. We were in the middle of a jungle complete with buffalo and other assorted jungle critters.

Morgan Vaux recalls the railroads; "Mr. Sun, my interpreter, my cook and I boarded the train, a narrow gauge railroad that ran between Iliang (my radio outpost) and Kunming. The train had several open sided cars pulled by an antique steam engine with "Paris 1901" clearly cast on each side of the boiler. The open sided cars had benches running the length of the car. Passengers sat everywhere, on benches, floors, and

Water buffalo.

roofs. Chickens and a few ducks were brought on board. Passengers loudly complained when the conductor came by collecting tickets.

On the car roofs, enterprising Chinese cooks cooked rice on charcoal brazers. Customers would reach up and the cooks would pass the rice down to outstretched hands. When the train approached a steep incline, passengers got off without complaint. The engineer would throw sand on the tracks for traction, and if needed, passengers would push the train up the incline to level ground. During these frequent stops, we could buy hard boiled eggs, also products of roof top cooking."

August 17, 1941
Went to try out my .45, it's OK. Walked to the RAF airdrome where our P-40s are parked. They have

quite a few modifications. The pilots went back to Rangoon in the Beechcraft to ferry more P-40s back to Toungoo. The airdrome is guarded by Burmese soldiers, Gurkas, and these guys are good. To the north of us are some mountains. Seventy miles beyond the mountains are the Japanese airfields. That's what we were told. We are 170 miles from Rangoon, 275 miles from Mandalay. It's raining now. It rains everyday.

I don't exactly recall what I meant in the diary when I wrote about "modifications," but Carl Quick, one of our mechanics, has a good story. He says our AVG P-40s were originally built for the British under Roosevelt's Lend-Lease program. The British P-40

We lined the parked ships up in staggered formation about 20-30 feet apart.

Another shot of the staggered formation.

versions had been modified with the full throttle position rearward. U.S. versions however had the full throttle position forward. Carl tells us about an experience starting a "British version" P-40. He set the throttle to almost full back (typical start position for the U.S. version). Next he fired the engine which immediately went full speed. The P-40 jumped the wheel chocks, and almost smashed before he got it under control. One hell of a scare he claims—no doubt.

Gurka soldier.

Shooting the .45.

The Gurkas had a fierce fighting reputation and were professional soldiers in every respect. As I recall we never had a security problem in Toungoo.

The .45 was not part of the "uniform." Dan Hoyle writes in the official 3rd Pursuit diary, "Men practicing with pistols and rifles on birds and most every moving thing. Bullets are whizzing all over the place. Fortunately no one gets hurt."

William Pawley's general purpose aircraft hauled everything—pilots, supplies, and the CAMCO president.

The Beechcraft.

August 18, 1941

Had our first squadron meeting at Toungoo. Hodges and I, along with some other good fellows have been assigned to C flight. C flight picked up 3 more P-40s. That makes 6. Jake and I hired a couple of guides and went "tiger hunting." Went 12 miles into a hot steamy jungle. All we shot was a duck. So much for "tiger hunting." Will go into the hills in a few days. The hills are about 117 miles away. I understand there's all kinds of wild game there. It's 8:30, the bugs are thick, and so are the locusts.

The P-40 aircraft was packed in a 30' X 8' crate consisting of the fuselage, wings, engine, tail section, and propeller. The single wing piece had replaceable wing tips. No guns, no radios. We put those in at Toungoo. I believe most of the aircraft were assembled in Rangoon by CAMCO, the Chinese, and some of our own people.

Bugs were everywhere and what little insect repellent we had didn't work very well. Eventually, I got used to the bugs. In Kunming the cold weather killed most of the critters by late September.

Hunting was a popular past time. No one from our group ever saw a tiger, much less shoot one.

Pagodas are Buddhists churches—they were everywhere.

Left to right: myself, Midge, Myet, and Myno, our houseboys.

August 19, 1941

It's been raining since 2 pm. It is damp in the evenings. Things mold very fast. Our official title is the First American Volunteer Group (AVG). We have native boys to do the work, the beds, shoes, and anything else. I'm getting tired of the mess stew, so went to Toungoo to get some food, cheese and crackers. It was great for a change. The exchange rate is $1.00 = 3 1/2 rupees Burmese. $1.00 = 2.13 Singapore $s. We were told to be careful before going to bed. Shake out the covers to get rid of any unfriendly company. We also had mosquito netting. It doesn't get cold in Toungoo. Most you need at night is a sheet. Quite comfortable. Lots of spiders, scorpions, centipedes and snakes. We have a small canteen (mostly toiletries and candies). First come first served, otherwise you are out of luck.

The boys did everything; the beds, laundry, shoes, most of the shopping, and even the haircuts. First time in my life someone waited on me, rather than the other way around. The service was heady stuff. Made me feel real important.

Midge was the #1 house boy and not much older then myself. He was a smart kid. I wonder what happened to him.

Both officer and enlisted ate in the same mess. The mess served curried stew seven days a week. Usually the curry was served with rice.

The canteen was small and stocked with cigarettes, razors, and some food stuffs.

Snakes, centipedes, and spiders were everywhere including the thatch. Once a scorpion bit a chap who crawled into his sheet covers before shaking them out. The bite made him quite sick. As I recall there wasn't

Kyedaw dining hall. Note the white tablecloths and spiffy waiters.

much Doc could do for scorpion bites. We were warned to shake out our shoes and socks before using them. Morgan Vaux also recalls the vermin; "One evening, when I was up at the radio station, the Chinese soldiers threw a victory celebration of some sort. I had many toasts of Saki wine. After the party I collapsed in my cot wearing my leather jacket. The next morning rats had eaten through the jacket and bit my arm in several places. The bites became infected and my arm swollen. They sent me back to Kunming for treatment."

August 20, 1941
Worked from 8:00 AM until 4 pm. Dinner from 1:00 PM until 2:00. Worked all day on ship #24, prop and valves. I work on ship #09 tomorrow. Ship #24 eventually went to Burgard. I don't know who flew #09.

The propeller.

Another propeller view.

The prop check consisted of tightening down the propeller hub with an oversized wrench. Next we checked the prop for balance and track and also checked the thrust bearing for tightness. Last, we checked the prop hub rear cone for galling (chafing). Galling was often caused by engine vibration. Frank Andersen recalls the time when Pete Atkinson flew a P-40 with a damaged propeller. "One of our ground crew had accidentally fired off a round and hit one of blades putting a bulge in the back side of it. In the States we would have rejected the prop, but in China props were hard to get. Pete suggested we try it out, so we tied the tail down and ran the engine up. The ship didn't vibrate any more then usual, so Pete took it up on a test hop. It seemed OK, so we flew the ship with that bulged prop, strictly against regulations."

Each aircraft had two numbers, a serial # and a squadron #. Most of the AVG serial numbers were in the 8,000s. My squadron numbers (the 3rd—Hell's Angels) started in the high 60s and ran through the 90s.

The valves were checked every 100 hours. Once the valve covers were removed, we visually inspected the valves for burns and warping. We checked compression by listening for air passing by the leaky valve. Valves were adjusted .015" for intake and .020" exhaust, same as a standard V8 engine.

August 21, 1941
Worked all day to get 3 P-40s in the air. P-40 #24 has a rusty thrust bearing. Boy, do they send them

The C15 engine. Note the engine banks and valve covers. The carburetor is attached to the back of the engine.

through the ringer. The Beechcraft flew in from Rangoon at 3:30 with the Major and the payroll. Still no letters from home. It started raining hard at 4:30. We have no water for showers so I stripped and took it in the rain—quite pleasant. This is roughing it. The chows rugged, too. Still the stew. Clothes cost 43r/3k for 2 khaki shirts, 20/4 for slacks, 2 khaki shorts for 9r, 1 white shorts 4r, 1 white shirt 3r.

Starting the Allison C-15 engine began in the cockpit. I adjusted the seat for a clean view of out the side of the cockpit (couldn't see forward because the airplane's nose was up). Next, I made sure the three way ignition switch was off—I didn't want the engine to accidentally fire-up and run over someone. I'd open the throttle and have someone pull the prop through a couple turns by hand. The propeller pull-through circulated the oil and got the gas flowing. Back in the cockpit, I turned the carburetor heat "off" and opened the radiator flaps. The closed radiator flaps helped the engine "warm up," but if they were accidentally left closed, the engine would overheat. Next, I'd pull the throttle back and "crack it"—just a little forward. Set the mixture control to "idle cut off." Turn the electric propeller switch "on," and set the prop

pitch to low. (The "low" setting helped avoid excessive "prop wash.") Next I selected a fuel tank—left wing, right wing, or fuselage. It was my choice, the pilots didn't care just as long as their tanks were full. Next I operated the "wobble pump" a strange contraption located on the center instrument panel between the pilot's legs. I would pump until the fuel pressure gauge started to rise. At higher field eleva-

Starting the Allison engine.

tions like Kunming, it was easy to over prime the engine and cause it to "backfire." Last I turned the ignition switch to "both on," yelled "clear" and toggled the "starter" switch. The starter switch spun up a large flywheel. Once the flywheel reached a certain RPM an automatic clutch engaged the engine. The engine would cycle 2 or 3 times before it fired. Once the engine was going I'd release the "starter switch" and move the "mixture control" from "idle cut off" to "automatic rich." As the engine "caught," it created a sensational mellow rumbling sound like a couple of V8 engines running in tandem. As the engine continued to catch, I watched the fuel pressure and at the same time checked the exhaust for signs of burning fuel. Burning exhaust usually signaled an over primed engine and almost certain backfire. Some of that black unburned gas and oil smoke always ended up in the cockpit—most unpleasant but quite memorable. Once the engine was running, I'd check the cooling flaps and electrical generators. If the oil pressure hadn't come up in 30 seconds, I'd stop the engine by pulling the mixture control back to the "idle cut-off" position and shut off the ignition. The "start" process took about 5 minutes. Starting the Allison C-15 engine was fun and something I enjoyed.

Performance was rated in terms of "input manifold pressure" (the pressure generated by the fuel/air mixture going into the engine), not engine rpm as in the case of an automobile or a fixed pitch propeller aircraft. Normally, the higher the manifold pressure, the greater the engine performance. Naturally, the pilots wanted lots of manifold pressure, but too much destroyed the engines, which were normally set to operate at 58 hg, the "take-off" position. The pilots wanted 62 hg. I recall we could make one small adjustment to improve engine performance. We could lengthen the "regulator" to "carburetor" rod by some number of turns, supposedly to "correct small manifold pressures." This "unauthorized " adjustment increased the aircraft speed and performance—just a little. The carburetor idling speed mixture adjustment was the only other adjustment we made on the C15 Allison.

Thrust bearings are big ball bearings located aft of the propeller shaft. We had to pull the prop to replace the bearings. The bearings would rust because of high humidity, the location of the bearings, and infrequent engine operation. It took our Navy mechanics a few tries before they could remove a prop without tearing the guts out of the Curtiss prop governor (contact points).

During the rainy season I'd grab a bar of soap, run outside, soap up, let the rain wash me off and jump into a clean set of clothes. Quite refreshing.

Cleanliness is next to Godliness.

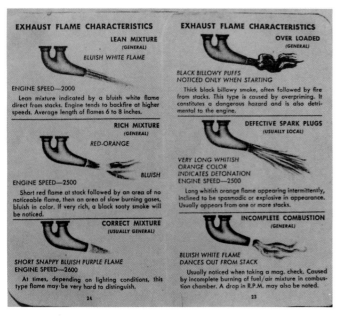

Once the engine started we "tuned" it by sight, sound, and smell. A properly running engine had a distinctive "mellow" sound, a clean "exhaust" smell, and a "bluish" color coming from the stacks.

August 22, 1941

More P-40s came in today. The Colonel gave us a talk. Tomorrow we sign up with the Chinese Air Force just for our own protection. Got my first letter since I left the States almost two months ago.

The Colonel talked about the importance of signing up with the Chinese Air Force. Most of it had to do with capture and the protection afforded under the Geneva Convention. I signed the following paragraph as did the rest of my comrades, but I can't remember "officially" becoming a member of the Chinese Air Force, nor can I remember getting any formal paperwork from the Chinese government.

"I hereby volunteer for service with the American Volunteer Group for duty in the Far East from July 4, 1940 to July 4, 1941. During this period I promise to render loyal service to the Group and obey the orders of my superior officers. It is understood that this voluntary offer of my services to the American Volunteer Group does not void or affect my contract with CAMCO in any way. After the termination of my services, I will not reveal any information relating to military matters which I have gained during my service." /s/ Frank S. Losonsky

Some AVG members also added the following:

"The above agreement is signed with the understanding that in addition to its not voiding or affecting my contract with CAMCO, that it further does not alter or change my present status as that of a Citizen of the United States, as regards any possible connection with the United States Army, Navy, or Marine Corps, or the Military Service of any other Country during the above stated period of the agreement."

It took about a month for the mail to arrive. I received about six or seven letters when I was with the AVG. Our mail was not censored.

August 23, 1941

Two more P-40s came in this morning. One had a rusty thrust bearing. Started work on it at 10:45 AM. Went to the market in Toungoo. The women wear

Toungoo village.

little clothing. The small boys and girls are nude and dirty. They say Calcutta is worse—that's hard to believe.

Betel nut was a popular narcotic used by men and women mostly of the poor class. Street vendors sold a combination of the reddish orange crushed nut, mixed with cocaine and wrapped in a coca leaf. The

Toungoo Market: Pictures are worth a thousand words. I still remember the smell.

combination was chewed much like a plug of tobacco. After the user finished the chew, the combination was spit out. Most users had stained red teeth. I never tried the stuff although I understand it had quite a kick. Other drugs were available. Morgan Vaux recalls. "A couple of old Mandarin Chinese invited Mr. Sun (my Chinese interpreter) and myself to an opium den. I tried a few puffs on a water pipe that was burning

Local Transportation: The natives carted their goods to market. Those who could afford the fare rode in rickshaws. For a few kopek the drivers took you anywhere.

some tar-like substance. The room became dense with smoke and the old men began to drift in and out of a trance. Sun and I left soon after that. I had nightmares that night."

Toungoo School: The school was located in the outskirts of town.

August 24, 1941
Jake, Frank Andersen, and I went hunting today. Shot a hawk, and a jungle dove. Damn near got lost. Finally got back at 11 am. Rained in the PM. The water is quite high. Talked with the Colonel this PM. He is quite a fellow. I've changed my pay to $300 home and $50 here. Muggy and hot tonight. Phonograph's going and they're playing some good music.

Hunting dove.

Jake and I just wandered off and got lost. It was a humbling experience. Fortunately a P-40 making practice landings at a nearby landing field helped us find our way back. I hunted mostly with a shotgun.

During the monsoon season, the water made a mess out of the aircraft taxi areas. I don't recall it flooding the runway or coming into the barracks.

August 25, 1941
Worked half a day today. We decided to take the mess and the bar over. The Colonel agreed. Rained this afternoon. Went to Toungoo. Ate steak at the railroad station for 5 rupees. Rodewald got ptomaine poisoning had to be hospitalized. It's very damp. The leather gets moldy overnight. God, what mold. Leather boots virtually rot overnight. It does some good to wipe the mold off first thing in the morning, but miss a couple days and you can forget about getting the stuff off.

Dampness got into everything. If leather wasn't protected it rotted. I had to brush the leather and air out of the clothes frequently, otherwise they smelled. We had no closets. The clothes hung on nails or a small clothesline strung in our bunk area.

The British and Soviet forces enter Iran, ostensibly to protect the oil fields. The British move on Abadan and Kermanshah, the Soviets move on Tabriz and both sides of the Caspian Sea. Little Iranian resistance is encountered. On August 29 Iran accepts armistice terms (see Richard Stewart's *Sunrise at Abadan*).

August 26, 1941

Went to the dentist today. Had a tooth filled. My jaw was numb all morning. I was quite sick so didn't go to work. Went to Toungoo at 4:30 pm. Had a steak and bought an album for the pictures. Our P-40s in Rangoon were sabotaged. They found sand in the oil and some loose rudder bolts. That will delay their arrival. My suit is moldy, so gave it to the boy. Ralwes (a small department store) was closed so couldn't get my suitcase. Bought a "bush" jacket and film for 45 rupees ($16.50).

Doc Bruce, an AVGer, did my dental work. I still have some of his handiwork in my mouth. Good work, Doc.

August 27, 1941

Changed out a directional gyro on Van's #15 ship. Doc put a temporary filling in today. Will get the rest of the filling Monday. Bought a suitcase at Ralwes for 36 rupees. Chinese General is coming tomorrow. He sent 50 qts of Bells' scotch whiskey and 50 lbs of chocolates. I took some of it to the RAF boys who have seen action. They are stationed here for "rest" duty.

Changing out a directional gyro required removal of four screws and a vacuum hose—not a tough job.

The cockpit is enclosed and has three sections of laminated glass. Behind the windscreen there was a section of 1.5 inch "bulletproof" glass. The cockpit

P-40 cockpit instrument panel.

P-40 cockpit

cover slid front and back for entry and exit. An emergency handle could release the entire sliding section. An emergency exit was available on the left side in case the plane turned over. A reinforced structure behind the pilot protected him in the event of a turnover.

We didn't mix much with the RAF. They stayed on their side of the field and we on ours. What little socializing we did with the British crew chiefs were cordial. The RAF boys appreciated the candy mentioned in the diary.

The Selfridge Field gang with their bottles of scotch.

August 28, 1941

Had an organizational talk by William Pawley [CAMCO's President] and a few other Chinese Generals. Worked in the AM only. Went to Toungoo, bought 5 rolls of film. I got my boots, quite comfortable. I wish we'd get some letters from home.

I never ran out of film when I was in China. As I recall film was about 3R ($.75) a roll.

Pawley briefed us on the squadron and hangar chief assignments.

August 29, 1941

They gave me P-40 #8119 (#71). I pulled my initial inspection. I took the engine cowling off and checked all the fluids, the lines, and tightened the spark plugs. They will put the guns and radios in this pm. Got my check from the Army for clothing. $13.96. Midge the boy has been telling me his troubles. He is a very intelligent young man about 21-22 years old.

My first ship was #8119 (#71) piloted by Ed Overend. Ed was a quiet fellow and a good pilot. He finished the AVG with 6 kills.

My ships had two 30 cal rifle caliber guns mounted in each wing panel and two 50cal cannon mounted on the cowl. The wing gun charging handles were located beneath the instrument panel. The ammunition boxes could hold 500 rounds per gun. The trigger switch was located on the stick. The 50cal ammunition came loose and had to be linked together. The armorers cleaned the guns as part of the preflight activities.

Covered 30cal wing guns. Stiles standing beside a "Hell's Angel."

The typical daily engine inspection consisted of checking spark plug wires and tightening fuel lines (identified with red bands near each union). After 5 hours we cleaned the carburetor fuel filter and checked

Two 50cal Cannon on either side of the carburetor air intake. Another view of the propeller, radiator, and gun sight.

Engine inspection in the jungle.

the engine idle. The idle adjustment knob was on the left side of the carburetor. We adjusted the idle for about 625 RPM. After 25 hours we inspected the spark

plugs for fouling. At 50 hours we would grind down the pits on the distributor rotor and clean and regap the spark plugs. At 100 hours we replaced the spark plugs—if we had them.

The radios were added after we arrived in Burma, plain RCA commercial jobs. The setup consisted of three boxes, a transmitter, a receiver, better in the evening, the higher frequency was better in the day. The radios operated air to air and air to ground. The radio men hated the installation. They crawled into a baggage compartment located behind the pilot's seat in 120+ degree heat then hauled the installation gear in. The work was tough. Part of the installation required running an antenna from the tail back to the baggage compartment. The installation took about 20 minutes on a cool day. On hot days, considerably longer.

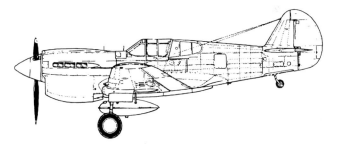

The radio was located behind the pilot. Note the baggage door slightly behind the canopy.

The Army clothing check finally caught up with me in Burma. As it turned out the AVG provided little clothing. They gave us gloves, a leather jacket and some overalls. We had no "standard" uniform code, nor did we stand dress inspection.

The uniforms (Above and next page)

Pilots Ed Overened and Erick Shilling flew ship #71.

The missionaries' pep talk about the virtues of "clean living" was mostly a scare tactic but it had some effect. I did little fooling around when I was over there.

August 31, 1941
Went to church, confession, communion at the Catholic church in Toungoo. The inside was homely, but nice. Only one Navy crew chief in the 3rd Pursuit. (We want an all Air Corps Squadron.)

The Catholic church was surprisingly well attended considering that Catholics were a minority in Burma. Church was very much part of my life in China.

The Toungoo barracks. Note the woven bamboo slats, which was surprisingly water resistant.

August 30, 1941
Worked till noon on #8119 (#71). The guns are in. They put the radios in Monday. General Won Fong Uit, a Chinese Air Force General, gave each of us a bottle of Bell's Scotch. In the PM some American missionaries invited me to their house for dinner. The food was good. Drank 4 cups of "real" coffee, the first I'd had since I left the Jaegersfontein. Found out that 75% of the people have syphilis and 65% have gonorrhea. The people are not to be fooled with. Seven of the pilots are going back to Rangoon to pick up more aircraft.

September 1, 1941
Moved to barracks 6 with most of the fellows from Selfridge Field. We lost "the Navy."

It's ironic—I spent over 29 years as an Allison technical representative doing Navy related things. I worked on their aircraft, served aboard their aircraft carriers, worked at their air stations and on occasions helped Naval Special Operations. I worked with a fine bunch of Navy folks.

September 2, 1941
Got paid today. Paid my 60 R mess bill. Also got a $50.00 U.S. bank draft. #8119 (#71) flew for the first time.

A P-40 fly over.

September 3, 1941
I've had it. Worked all day in 120 degree heat. I think we are going to work mornings. I hope so, because it is so hot. Got word that the Japanese have bombed Loiwing, our about to be new home. Apparently all was destroyed including the nice dorm that Madame Chiang had set up for us. We are getting organized, and should be hitting the road soon. Got my pass for Mandalay.

Madame always had a soft spot for the AVG. She believed that the AVG would help the Chinese people fight harder.

September 4, 1941
My ship is grounded for a 5 hour inspection. Went to Toungoo for dinner and made a reservation for Mandalay—14 rupees. We leave on the 10:00 PM train, travel all night, arrive Mandalay in the AM. The boy made us some good coffee. We have it just about every night.

We checked the ignition shields, oil lines, and cooling lines for vibration damage.

September 5, 1941
Had some trouble getting off to Mandalay. We were booked with some "undesirables," so decided to go first class. Cost us 28/5/6 ($8.00) vs. 14/2/9 for second class. Two of our ships cracked up. One coming in for a landing ran into the other. Sandell into Bacon. Both in B flight. One ship totally out of commission.

The Leadership. (L-R Chiang Kai-Shek, Madame Chiang Kai-Shek, Claire Chennault)

Sandell and Bacon's wreck—Bacon's ship.

Another view. It's a wonder they survived.

September 6, 1941

Arrived Mandalay in the AM. Met Mr. Sassman at the station. He took us to some shops where I bought an opal ring (35 rupees, $10.00), jade ring (45 rupees, $13.00), and some teak wood and ivory carvings. Also got some stamps and coins. Saw the palace at Mandalay and the Mandalay Hill. Both beautiful. Left Mandalay at 6 PM, arrived Toungoo at 2:30 in the morning.

Mandalay was a beautiful place for rest and relaxation (above and next).

September 7, 1941

The fellows were impressed with the rings, gems, and the carvings. They want to go next time. Went bike riding.

Everyone had a bicycle. I bought a standard British BSA—highly reliable. I never had a breakdown, not even a flat tire. I bought the BSA in Toungoo for $35. Most of my bike riding was around the base or Toungoo, a couple of miles away. Bikes were used

strictly for transportation. No one worried about biking alone. It was safe everywhere. Morgan Vaux recalls, "Nearly everyone bought bikes in Toungoo in order to get to the only 'western' food in the area—at the Toungoo railroad station. The station had beer, steak sandwiches and a coolie operating a ceiling fan by pulling on this line connected to the fan."

Bicycle—Morgan Vaux.

We salvaged what little remained of Armstrong's airplane. Sad sight.

September 8, 1941
A disastrous day for the B flight. Armstrong (Army) and Bright's ships collided in mid-air. Bright bailed out, Armstrong went down with the ship. Couldn't tell it was Army, he was all messed up. One of the most sociable Navy pilots I knew. Army was single. Bright survived with a few scratches. That makes 4 aircraft from B flight in 3 days.

September 9, 1941
We worked 1/2 day. The afternoon was set aside for Armstrong's service. It was very nice. I didn't do much, went to town. We killed a foot long viper outside our barracks in the afternoon. The native boys said it's dangerous.

Vipers were common around the barracks, especially after a hard rain. The snakes liked the high ground. The boys would kill at least one a month. I don't believe any of our people were ever bit by a snake.

September 10, 1941
Worked hard all day. My ship (#71) flew 4 hours. Summer and the dry season is here, and it is hot. I hope we move soon. I bought some mugs today.

The dry season started in September and lasted until the beginning of the monsoon season in May. The cloud formations were quite spectacular and it was possible to "time" the afternoon rains by the formations.

Summer cloud formations.

September 11, 1941
More dentists, more filled teeth, and more Novocain. The stuff makes me sick, so I stayed in the barracks. Starting tomorrow, we work 1/2 days only. It's too hot to work in the afternoons. We will start at 6:15 and work till noon. The fellows brought many things to eat from town.

Ducks and chickens were killed daily and hung up for sale.

September 12, 1941
Up at 4:30 AM and in the hangar by 6:00 to change my rudder and gas the ships. I had to gas all 7 ships today. It took the boys 65 minutes, or about 10 minutes per plane. It was 120 in the shade. I was wet all day. The 3rd Pursuit is really getting into a groove now.

Fueling Frank Swartz's #49 from a truck (Kunming China)

plate. The capacity of the three tanks was about 132 gallons. In Rangoon and Kunming trucks delivered fuel. The trucks could pump the gas but in outlining areas we had no trucks or truck pumps and much of the fuel was pumped by hand, from 55 gallon drums. The Chinese mechanics rolled the drums to the aircraft, set them on end and hand pumped the fuel into the aircraft. The gas was filtered before it went into the aircraft (also see January 13, 1942).

Fueling #49 (Kunming China)

The P-40s had three fuel tanks. One in the fuselage behind the pilot, and two in the wings. The fuselage filler cap was located behind the pilot's armor

Warming up #49 (Kunming China)

In Norway, the pro-German government bans the Boy Scouts. Elsewhere, Kiev, Russia falls to the Germans.

September 13, 1941
At work by 6 am. My ship flew first period. It went out with a bad tachometer. Had a tough time trying to get it out because of the location. Won't complete it until Monday. I feel like I'll hang one on tonight. It's been about 7 months since the last one. I'll do it up right. The fellows have set up a pole vaulting contest. I stand the highest so far at about 6'. I hurt my right side and foot. No work tomorrow.

Oil was stored in a 12.7 gallon tank in the fuselage behind and above the fuselage fuel tank. The coolant expansion tank was ahead of the firewall and contained 2 gallons of antifreeze. (L-R) Two natives, Van Timmerman, Losonsky.

The P-40 propeller.

Flying periods. (Above and Below)

As I recall the flying was staggered into three periods: Period 1 began early in the AM, period 2 late in the AM, and period 3 early in the PM.

The propeller was a Curtiss electric. Normally we checked the prop hub nut for tightness, then the thrust bearing. Next we checked the hub rear cone for galling and last, checked the prop blades for proper pitch setting.

If a prop struck an object or if the pilot noted any vibration, we checked the blade angle settings and the "propeller track." Checking the "track" was simple. First rotate one of the prop blades to the low point.

Place a box under the blade. Mount a wood splinter on the box beneath the blade tip. Rotate the prop until the next blade tip is above the wood splinter. Measure the distance between the wood and the blade. If the distance was more then 1/16 we were supposed to remove the prop and straighten it out. Removing a prop took several hours so many a propeller flew more then 1/16" out of track.

If excessive material was removed from one blade, as in the case of removing nicks or scratches, the propeller characteristics could be altered where the thrust of the blades were no longer equal. This condition invariably makes the blade revolve in a different plane of travel and sometimes caused vibration.

At 100 hours we removed the contact switch cover from the prop governor motor and checked the contacts.

Pole vaulter.

I was the #1 pole vaulter in the squadron, even though I didn't know what I was doing. I cleared 6' with a bamboo poll.

The monkey and Van Timmerman.

September 14, 1941
Went to church. Fourth Sunday in a row. Went to the bazaar in Toungoo. Pawley and the Colonel flew in from Rangoon on their way to Chungking. Still hot. We have a monkey mascot.

The monkey belonged to Carl Quick. What a monkey—and smart too. He'd get into rafters at night and keep us up. The monkey liked toothpaste and shaving cream. He'd squirt the stuff all over the place. One of our group, quite upset over the monkey's antics, shot him dead. Quite sad.

September 15, 1941
28 new fellows came in today. 20 pilots, 8 mechanics. We gave them a hardy welcome. Played "Home Sweet Home" as their train pulled into the station.

We were happy to see new faces from home. Several of the arrivals, after seeing their accommodations, got back on the train and went home.

September 16, 1941
Got my second ship today—#75. We boresight her tomorrow. Won't be long before we go North. It rained. First we've had in 8 days. It will be good sleeping weather tonight.

Boresighting—Setting the P-40 up. (Courtesy Don Rodewald)

My P-40s had four .30 caliber wing guns (2 .30s on each wing) and the 2 .50 caliber nose guns. Like

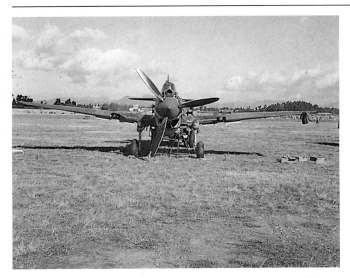

Boresighting—Straight on view of the setup. (Courtesy Don Rodewald)

Boresighting—Shooting at the target. (Courtesy Don Rodewald)

Boresighting—Leveling the P-40. (Courtesy Don Rodewald)

any weapon, the guns had to be aimed. The aiming process was called boresighting. As I recall, the process took several hours. We taxied the aircraft to a safety area. The armorers leveled the aircraft with wing and tail jacks. Sometimes we used the back end of a flat bed truck to raise the tail. The object was to simulate an aircraft in flight. The guns were fired one at a time into a target about 300 yards away. Each gun was adjusted until the bullet hit the target. The .30cal wing gun pattern was set to criss-cross about 250 yards in front of the aircraft. Tracer ammo was used to help the armorers aim the guns. Chuck Baisden, one of our armorers, describes the art of good boresighting in his book "Flying Tiger to Air Commando."

Carl Quick remembers the time when Eric Shelling was taxiing the aircraft out to the boresight range. He hit some mud and sank the ship right up to the belly. Couldn't budge the thing. Spent the rest of the day digging the ship out. No boresighting that day.

Otto Daube, a crew chief, told us that the British absolutely refused to let us boresight in late afternoon. The machine gun fire interfered with the peace and quiet of their "tea time."

Occasionally a pilot or ground crew would accidentally shoot off a round. I recall one incident in Loiwing when I was warming up an aircraft in the dark. Someone accidentally hit the trigger and sent tracers all over the field. What an impressive sight, but it scared the devil out of us.

September 17, 1941
The new pilots were checked out. Hedman joined our squadron. McMillan nosed one up. A sad sight. Went to Toungoo for supper. Had our first movie,

"Jesse James." They plan three movies a week. Cost 10 rupees a month.

Duke Hedman was a super pilot. We became good friends at Selfridge Field. On one memorable occasion he and I flew a AT-6 to Ashley, Michigan, to visit my future wife Nancy. As my wife recalls, "I was so excited because airplanes were not common in our area. Sometimes an enterprising pilot would show up and charge the locals a few dollars for a sky view of their farms, but few had the cash or the courage to go up. I remember I was in study hall when Frank Losonsky and Duke flew over. The airplane came in real low. We girls were quite excited as this crazy plane buzzed the high school twice or maybe it was three times. They made loud passes. I was thrilled, not many gals in that small town had the fun of having their boyfriend buzz them. Several weeks later Duke and Frank did it again, only this time at night. They followed the railroad tracks up to my house and set the

Nancy, my wife of many years.

engine into high pitch and flew low. My father was furious. He wanted to know what in the hell those idiots were doing up there. He claimed they were very unusual and quite crazy. Naturally, I was thrilled to death with their flying antics, which I don't think it helped the situation."

The P-40 was easy to "nose up." Too much brake on a rolling aircraft stood it straight on its nose. A

Nosed up Hurricane.

nose-up usually required replacement of the oil cooler, cooling flaps, and Prestone. Often the prop had to be replaced, usually a half day job, if parts were available.

September 18, 1941
Ships flew formation. Got my July pay of 150 rupees. Won 50 rupees shooting craps. Rained all day.

Flying formation.

September 19, 1941
Ships flew formation today. Practicing for tomorrow's review. Some senior officials coming in tomorrow. Had my big toe lanced today at the hospital—infection—probably from the pole jumping. I can hardly walk. Went to town tonight. Bought some crackers, cheese, and beans. It rained hard tonight.

The hospital was located at the end of the field. The facilities were adequate for most of our needs. Doc sent the serious cases to Rangoon. Doc and the nurses lived in the hospital complex. I don't believe the British used our medical facilities.

September 20, 1941
Today we had our air show. On display was a U.S. Hudson bomber all set for action, bombs, guns, etc.

"Commanders" watching the air show.

Also a British Blenheim. It looked like our B-10 only not quite as good. We also had a British General. Went to Toungoo in the PM. Won 60 R.

Note the "wicker chairs" in the Blenheim bomber—a hold over from WW I. Guess it saved weight.

September 21, 1941
Went to church. Bought an opal for 5 R ($1.42), a sapphire for 10 R ($2.85). Cost me 5 R to put it into a silver ring. Saw "Drums Along the Mohawk." Rained again.

Movies were a popular past time for pilots and ground crew alike. An absolute morale builder.

September 22, 1941
Today is a sad day. We lost another pilot—Hammer. He spun in. The natives said he was in an inverted

Hudson Bombers: The Hudson was built by Lockheed for the British RoyalAir Force.

flat spin. He went down 7 miles north of the field, off the road, in the jungle. They didn't find much of him. Got some mail from the States. It sure feels good.

Hammer's spin.

The airplane assumes an upside down spinning position on a horizontal axis. There is virtually no way the pilot can fall free from the aircraft. He rides the spinning aircraft down pushed against the floor of the cockpit.

Hammer

September 23, 1941
Hammer's funeral tomorrow. I'm very sick. I believe I have malaria. I went to see the Doc. He gave me some pills. He is going to check up on me tomorrow. It's raining again.

Doc Rich and Doc Gentry were good guys. They took care of us in Burma and China. After the war it was Doc Rich who recognized the ground crew for

our unique contributions. He passed away in 1992 and will be missed by all.

Doc Gentry

September 24, 1941
No ships flew—rain. Just as good because I was in the hospital all day. Doc said I had dysentery. Boy, it sure knocks the wind out of your sails. I feel very weak.

September 25, 1941
Got ship #74 today. The ships flew 3 hours. They are really bucking now because the time is nearing to leave Toungoo, and we are all set to go. I feel better today. Had a little moon, but it's 9:30 PM and it's gone now.

The Command had finished training. It was time to go. None of us realized it would be another three months before we left for China.

September 26, 1941
Little's plane ran off into the boondocks and nosed his ship up. Another one for "B" flight. Played baseball with the pilots and got beat.

Little's nose-up.

Little's nose-up. Another view.

Little's nose-up.

Although the ship looked like a washout it was relatively easy to repair. The prop and cooler took about 6 hours to replace, the left landing gear another 6 hours.

September 27, 1941
"A" flight nosed one over today. Went to Kline's for

dinner. No rain today but it was 109 degrees. I burned my hand checking the left bank of spark plugs.

Kline's was a popular Toungoo hangout. It was a great place to find out what was going on in the area. The Klines were the local intelligence agency. They had information on everything.

September 28, 1941
Went to church. Bought a ruby for 100 rupees. Am having it put in a gold ring. Went to the movie "Boom Town." The flies and mosquitoes are plenty thick now.

End on view of spark 'intake' plugs, harness, and intake manifold.

The C15 engine, another view.

The bugs weren't near as bad in China. We used mosquito netting at night to keep the critters off.

September 29, 1941
Ships flew one mission. The ceiling was 500 feet. The weather was X (bad). It cooled down after raining all afternoon. I think CAMCOs is going to pay for our chow. Least I hope so.

September 30, 1941
Got ship #71 out from a 25 hour inspection. Runs like a top. Biked to town. It's quite a paddle. Rained hard today. I think we'll get a new contractor for the mess. Another month, another $350. Trouble is that CAMCO doesn't pay on time.

The 25 hour inspection consisted of: 1) checking the ignition shielding, 2) cleaning the carburetor fuel strainer, 3) checking all oil lines, 4) checking the cooling lines for leaks, 5) checking the four engines hold down nuts and bolts, 6) checking valve clearances and the propeller, 7) doing all daily inspections.

The food was bad and we were sick of Indian cuisine. We wanted a menu change.

The pay was correct but arrived months late. CAMCO had to bring the payroll in from who-knows-where.

The laundryman (dobie).

October 1, 1941
Paid today. A $50 bank draft and the rest in rupees. Went to town. Bought 6 "T" shirts 5 rupees ($1.42), 1 dozen handkerchiefs 3 rupees ($.85), 1 long 1 short pants and 6 shirts for 19/8 rupees ($5.57). Laundry cost me 1/14 R ($.42) this week.

The wash was done by a "dobie," a washerman. As I recall he picked the laundry up twice a week in the morning, and returned it a couple of days later. The dobies did a good job on our clothes.

October 2, 1941
Got our July pay today. Have a beautiful moon tonight. It's the first time it's been like this. There was a Navy Brewster here today. One of the British pilots really put it through the (acrobatic) ringer.

Moscow is attacked by the Germans.

Brewster Buffalo—front and side views.

October 3, 1941
Worked hard today. Biked into town. Am having silver butts made for the gun. I ate a quart and a half of ice cream at the railroad station.

The railboy. He manually switched the trains from one set of tracks to another.

The railroad station was a popular eating place. The ice cream was delicious.

October 4, 1941
Today is the Burmese New Year. They sure use lots of fireworks to celebrate. Biked to town.

The celebration and fireworks lasted all night.

October 5, 1941
Church at 6:30. Ate at the railroad station. Saw a movie. Harold Osborne came in from Rangoon today. It was hot today. The moon is big tonight. It sure brings back memories.

October 6, 1941
We have 55 ships now for three squadrons. Had 9 flying today, the most yet. We're getting into gear

Part of the Toungoo flight line.

now. Got a pair of shorts, long pants, 6 shirts for 23 R. It's mild and cool tonight.

October 7, 1941
Lost another ship from "A" flight, and nosed one up. The pilot, Schiel, bailed out and landed in the jungle, in a swamp and almost drowned. He was scratched up a bit, but nothing serious. Had an electrical storm, and plenty of rain. Bought a French sapphire stone for 9 R.

Schiel's bail-out job.

Schiel, another view.

October 8, 1941
My Birthday, I'm 21 today. I am a "man." Took my gun in to get it "blued." I've got three ships now. Went to Toungoo on a bike.

My 21st birthday was pretty special. As I recall the fellows bought me a beer. I was legal now.

October 9, 1941
Because we only work 1/2 day all three ships keep me plenty busy. A few of the fellows have gone up the road to Kunming. Two more leave tonight. The

radio and photo folks. Lost 130 rupees ($37.14) playing poker and blackjack. Muggy tonight. Movie "They Drive By Night."

Gambling was a popular pastime. Losing 130 R in a night was a big loss. It didn't happen often. I was a fair poker player.

October 10, 1941
No flying today. Saw "Babes in Arms." Am having a clip case made for my .45.

The native craftsman were great carvers. They made anything you wanted, cheap and high quality. The most popular items were the water buffalo carvings.

October 11, 1941
Inspection today. 38 new fellows came in today, including Newell. Went out to see Frank Schiel's bail out job for some pictures.

Roll call was the closest we came to a formal inspection.

October 12, 1941
Missed church today. Got "canned up." Played poker last night. It was hot. I have been thinking of the States a lot today.

"Canned up" was slang for drinking. We drank mostly on the weekends. I don't recall much drinking on the job. The natives brewed a potent whiskey called Mekong—quite popular. The missionaries made gin out of rice and juniper berries—potent. In Toungoo, we drank scotch. We also visited the railroad station where they served a "Jaffa" beer in liter bottles. Sat around the station and told lots of lies. The Burmese also served a rum in a 7Up size bottle called "Tiger Balm." They claimed the stuff was 200 proof—very potent. At Mingaladon they served an Aussie ale. One bottle was enough to get smashed. The Brits also served warm gimlets. We had horrible beer in Kunming.

"Thinking of the States" was frequent pastime. I'd been in country 3 months and missed the things that come natural to a 21 year old—like girls.

October 13, 1941
Ships flew 3 missions. It rained after they returned. The fellows are getting fed up and pi—ed off at the whole works. I'm getting that way too. Maybe it will blow over.

October 14, 1941
We warmed the ships up in the rain. No flying. Two new crew chiefs arrived, so I gave up one of my ships. Still have two.

Warmup

"Warmup." Note the 55 gallon gas drums. I hope they were empty. An exhaust spark could set the works off.

We did most of the aircraft warmups (runups) in early morning. Before the "startup" I checked the tires for cracks and bulges and pulled the pito tube cover off. Next I drained water and crud from the gas sumps and checked the hydraulic landing struts for leaks or broken seals. If an aircraft landed "hard" on bad struts it usually damaged the landing gear and sometimes bent a prop. I'd pull the rudder chocks then check the control surfaces (ailerons, rudder, elevator, flaps) from the cockpit. Last I checked the fuel tanks. If the windshield was dirty I'd clean it with water. The armorers would check the guns during the "runup."

The radio men usually checked the radios and set the frequencies hours earlier. The radios were checked off the internal aircraft batteries so they didn't need the engine running.

Next I'd taxi the aircraft to a runup for a series of checks before I turned the ship over to the pilot. First the instruments. Oil pressure gauge should read between 15 and 60 lbs. Oil temperature about 40 C (warmed up). Next I increased the engine RPM to check for "roughness." I checked the two magnetos by revving the engine up to 2300 rpm. I switched between the two magnetos. If the RPM dropped more then 100 it usually meant a bad spark plug or a magneto problem.

It was easy to miss a bad cylinder, so I checked the flames coming out of the exhaust stacks, all 12 of them, to make sure the cylinders were firing. The damp weather often caused moisture to collect in the distributor head which caused rough running engines. The trick was to keep them dry.

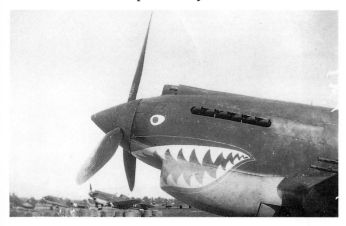

The propeller and exhaust stacks.

The prop check was simple. Move the prop control from "low" to "high," watch for a drop in RPM and listen to the propeller "bite" into the air.

Before the pilot took over, one last quick gauge check: oil inlet temperature (85-104 F), oil pressure (idle 15 lbs min), coolant outlet temperature (85-185 F), and fuel pressure (16 lbs min). As I recall the instruments were "red lined" with paint so it made the checks easier.

The whole process took about 30 minutes. I must have done a few things right—all my pilots returned. I only recall one problem: Ken Jernstedt's engine was running rough on a trip from Kweilin to Lowing. A new set of spark plugs fixed the problem.

Spark plugs were rare commodities in Burma and China. What we couldn't steal, we salvaged, cleaned, and reconditioned many times over. When an engine "idled" for long periods, oil and lead deposits "loaded up" the spark plug electrodes and caused the engine to run "rough." In combat the P-40 pilots often flew the ships "hot and rich." This "hot-rich" engine condition blew oil by the rings and "loaded up" the plugs. If the "load up" wasn't bad, we "blew" it out by speeding up the engine and pulling power (increase propeller pitch). The only other way to "fix" fouled plugs was to remove them, brush and wash them—a tedious task. Each cylinder had two spark plugs. I always made sure we had at least one "good" plug per cylinder. We gapped the spark plugs at .012." The C-15 Allison engine came with Champion C-34-ses or AC LS-85s (ceramic) plugs.

If an engine overheated it would sometimes crack the ceramic spark plugs. Cracked spark plugs were a pain to remove. It was tricky getting the little broken pieces out of the cylinder well without dropping them into the spark plug hole. Sometimes a mechanic over torqued a plug and broke it off in the cylinder. What a mess, because we had to drill the spark plug out then retap the cylinder hole.

October 15, 1941
My pilots, Hedman and Martin, have ships #74 and #71. They flew 3 missions. Biked to town got my clip case 3/8/0 rupees. Gun (.45) hasn't come back yet. Saw "Maryland" (movie).

October 16, 1941
Worked till 10:30 AM then back to work at 2:30 pm. Had a review for Lady Duff-Cooper. The bugs are really bad now that the dry season has set in.

I don't remember who Lady Duff-Cooper was, much less why we put the show on. The bugs were a bigger problem.

October 17, 1941
Ship #71 came in with a restricted oil valve. The pilot was all oil. Played a game of volleyball, lost three games. Harold Osborne and one of the other boys had a bald head haircut.

Propeller shaft thrust bearings are behind bolted down ring.

A restricted oil valve could destroy an engine quick. As I recall, the valve was located in the oil pump. We had to drain the engine, remove the pump, then replace the valve—a tedious job.

The daily oil inspection checked for leaks, and turned the Cuno oil filter through one full counterclockwise turn. The Cuno oil filtration device "cleaned" the oil by passing it through 2 fine mesh rotating filter disks. The filter disks were cleaned with gasoline or mineral spirits. After 50 hours the oil was changed, drained into 55 gallon drums. I'm sure the old oil ended up on the "black market." The stuff was still good for auto engines. We even used it in our trucks.

Haircuts

Volleyball was a popular team sport, but we didn't play it that often in the 100 degree heat and high humidity.

In China, the head was shaved. Appears some of our boys adopted the local custom. One sure way to get rid of lice was to shave the head. Osborn may have had a lice problem.

Tojo assumes the offices of prime minister, war minister, and home affairs minister. The Soviets evacuate Odessa, a naval port on the Black Sea. In Moscow, foreign diplomats leave along with much of the government.

October 18, 1941
Hot [weather]. Had 2 Japanese recon aircraft taking pictures of our base. The C.O. (Commanding Officer Olson) flew #74, my ship. Brake check for ship #71. Criz is the pilot. Went to town. Bought some canned goods. Went to the post show, saw "When Tomorrow Comes."

Olson was liked by the pilots early in the war. Thirteen days later P-40 #74 ended up on the scrap heap (see October 31, 1941).

Criz was a likeable fellow. He had his problems with the AVG and eventually went back to the States.

Criz next to his "Lady."

The brakes were similar to the standard drum brakes found on vintage '40, '50, or '60 automobiles. We checked the wheel cylinders and brake connections for leaking brake fluid.

The landing gear under Losonsky.

October 19, 1941
Went to church. Bought a gold chain and a medal from the priest for 30 rupees. It was hot but cooled down tonight. A Stenson 105 flew in from Rangoon. Col. sent the armorers down to (Rangoon) to arm 6 ships. We start roll call tomorrow.

October 20, 1941
Went to work at 6:30 am. We are on alert now, thanks to the two Japanese recon aircraft. We have 12 planes armed and ready to go at a moment's notice. The time is short now. The States are having a war scare on.

Alert meant that planes were armed, fueled, and parked in staggered patterns near the field. Before October 20 we came and went as we pleased. We showed up for work and didn't have to account for our whereabouts. We had no formal inspections. After October 20, we had formal roll calls. War was coming but we didn't know where, when, or how it would develop. There was lots of excitement back in the States. My sister Ann and my future wife Nancy wrote that lots of women were taking jobs in the war industries.

A British Blenheim bomber.

October 21, 1941
Very hot. Installed the bullet proof shield. Damn near passed out. 3 Blenheims came in. Our squadron intercepted them.

I had to remove the pilot's seat to bolt one of the bullet proof shields in place. As I recall they weighed about 50 lbs. The installation was a pain. The P-40 had three pieces of armor plate: one piece 7 mm. thick ahead of the pilot from the windscreen line down to the top of the engine, a piece 7 mm. thick behind the pilot's back, and 9 mm. thick behind his head. The armor plate had other uses—such as cooking grills. After the Rangoon mess closed down, Carl Quick "obtained" one of the plates and used it as a Bar-B-Q grill.

The British Blenheim bombers flew in from Rangoon as part of a mock attack. These practice attacks helped us test the Chinese early warning network. The network was made up mostly of Chinese "spotters" located throughout the country. Once "spotters" detected the incoming aircraft they notified headquarters. Headquarters in turn notified the squadrons. The network was also was used to guide lost pilots back to their air bases. On this day the warning network gave us enough time to launch a successful counter strike. We weren't so lucky on December 23rd and the 25th.

October 22, 1941
Hot weather. Played ball, won against the pilots. Ken Merritt lost his elevator and had to force land.

October 23, 1941
#67 cracked up today—Hodges. It was his first. We had our first air raid today. The Blenheims beat hell out of us.

October 25, 1941
It was foggy this morning, no flights off. About 9:05 Pete went up for a test hop. 15 minutes later we saw him coming down from 10,000'. At 4,000 the tail tore

Hodges' #67. View 1.

Hodges' #67. View 2.

October 24, 1941
I am on the alert crew. Got up at 4:00 AM. Boy what a sunrise. Moss nosed one up today. Movie tonight is "East Side of Heaven."

off and then the ship exploded. He was one of the best and most well liked pilots in the squadron. It burns me up to see him go. The motor made a hole 15' deep. The whole works was a mess.

We were on the flight line and heard the ship going into a power dive, not all that unusual. All of a sudden the noise stopped. When we looked up the wings were still floating down. Pete Atkinson and I attended church together. He was a good friend, one of those rare persons who took an interest in you. He was truly missed by all. We never found what caused the crash. I remember we sent the Chinese mechanics into that hole with instructions to salvage all they could. You did what you had to do to keep the other aircraft flying.

Sunrise. I still remember dawn breaking, and those early sunrises. To quote from Kipling: "The sun rose like thunder across the bay."

Pete Atkinson's accident.

Atkinson's engine.

funeral we returned to the barracks. The movie took the edge off the day. Pete's death reminded me how quickly it's over.

October 27, 1941
All ships grounded to check the tail and wing bolts. It was foggy but hot after the fog lifted. The rice is getting ripe.

After Pete's accident the ground crews checked the ships wing and tail bolts for fracture and wear. They were in good shape.

When the rice ripened it turned a brown color. Rice grew in ponds and was hand harvested.

Keith (Christensen) and I doing a different kind of "shooting" (a slingshot) this time for beer. I won.

October 26, 1941
Went to church. They buried Pete at 4:30. At 7:05 a (Japanese) ship came over. It was the first time the alert crew has seen action. A flight went up, but couldn't intercept it. It had a 20 mile head start. Movie: Joe Brown in "Flying High."

That Sunday in church I said a few prayers for Pete. The funeral was a tough, somber occasion (I hate funerals). I recall a simple box covered with the U.S. flag. Those of us who were not on alert attended. Our padre, Paul Frillman, conducted a small ceremony. The CO said a few words, I don't recall about what. The cemetery wasn't fancy. Pete was buried in the Church of England cemetery in Toungoo. After Pete's

October 28-29, 1941
Routine work.

October 31, 1941
Conant washed my ship (#74) out. McMillan's wing got clipped off [#76].

Liebold's ship was sitting at the end of the runway. McMillan was almost off the ground when his wing ran into Liebold's propeller. The prop cut McMillan's wing tip off. McMillan was able to fly the ship around the field and make a safe landing—amazing piece of flying, an amazing aircraft!

The Germans sink the U.S. destroyer "Ruben James" with loss of U.S. life.

Conant's washout. Conant flew PBMs (flying boats) before he joined the AVG.

McMillan's clipped wing. View 1. (Above)   *McMillan's clipped wing. View 2. (Below)*

November 1, 1941
Bought a bike for 111 rupees ($30), a sapphire for 20 rupees, silver gun butts 42 rupees. Won 400 rupees. Worked hard today. Hot again.

November 2, 1941
Went to church, communion. Went swimming in the mountains, then visited Dr. Cote, a woman doctor. Dr. Cote has been in Burma for 50 years. She got her medical degree in the US. She has delivered over 5,000 babies. She is 86 years old and still gets around. Also went to a tea factory. Altitude 4,169'.

Born in 1855, the Doctor was an impressive lady. Conversation centered on events of the day, mostly the coming war. I never saw her again.

November 3, 1941
Worst day of all. Conant nosed ship #78 in. Raine had a tire blow out on ship #80. It's a wash out (seriously wrecked). McAllister nosed #77 up. Blackburn ran ship #7 into #8. Sandell ground looped. Overley ran into ship #83 and washed out an aileron, and one ship had tail wheel trouble at Lashio.

Raine's #80.

Ship #7 and #8.

Conant's skid.

Reed's #79. View 1.

#79. View 2.

November 4, 1941
Reed nosed ship #79 over. Too hot a landing. That makes 6 wrecks in 3 days. Got high tonight.

Little, if any, official documentation exists about the accidents in November and early December 1941. For a time it appeared Chennault would run out of aircraft. Erik Shilling recalls, "By December 7, the AVG was down to 54 ships." 45 were either out of commission or wrecked. Few remember the dedicated ground force who put the wrecks back together and kept the 'Flying Tigers' flying.

November 5, 1941
Conant washed ship #81 out. That makes three in 5 days. I don't know what they will do with him now.

Conant checked out in #77 (L-R) Losonsky, Unknown, Conant.

November 6, 1941
They put me in engineering today. Got ship #85 out. I hope we go up the road soon. I'm getting sick of the heat. Movie: "Seven Summers." The moon is bright tonight—memories.

Engineering did all major repairs and modifications including engine changes. The crew chief often followed his aircraft into "engineering" for the 25 hour maintenance.

The Allison C15 was an easy engine to remove. Off came the spinner, prop motor, and the prop. Next we disconnected the wiring, fuel, and oil cooling lines. Four large bolts secured the engine to the frame. Once

Conant's #81. Conant's crew chief remarked "Beautiful landing 15' off the ground."

the bolts were removed, the engine could be lifted up and out with the help of a cable sling suspended from a large wooden tripod (or a thick tree branch). The sling hooks attached to the #1 and #7 right and left exhaust cylinder hold-down studs. As we pulled the sling tight the engine was pushed slightly forward, up, then out. Once out, we placed the engine in a stand. If the engine was going to Loiwing for major overhaul we crated it. The overhaul work at Loiwing was done by the Chinese under U.S. supervision. It took a couple of hours to pull an engine. The engines we received from the factory were pretested prior to shipment, so all we did is mount them, run them for a couple of hours, and check the magnetic oil plug for metal filings.

"Boneyard"—spare parts salvaged from aircraft. We kept everything that wasn't rusty, burned, or badly damaged.

November 7, 1941
Worked in the hangar all day. Kunming was bombed this afternoon. One of our ships is down in a rice paddy near Maymyo. Movie tonight is "Lady Eve Tonight."

The hangar.

The hangar was open on both ends—thank heavens, otherwise we'd roast to death. During the rainy season there was always a breeze. By mid afternoon the sun would heat the aircraft metal until it was impossible to work on them. Early morning was the best time to work on the aircraft.

November 8, 1941
Pulled a weekly on all the ships. Six Brewsters came in from Rangoon. Played volleyball against the staff. Took two straight. Biked to Toungoo.

We checked the batteries, landing gear struts, and tires.

November 9, 1941
Missed church today. Went swimming. Movie tonight is the "Third Finger Left Hand."

November 10, 1941
Foggy this morning. Two of our ships fired at ground targets.

The diary refers to a target practice range located some miles away and not an engagement with the Japanese forces. As I recall the cloth targets were about 5' square with "bull's eyes" painted on them. The cloth targets were placed in the middle of a field. The pilots practiced on the targets about twice a week. Duke Hedman was one of our better air to ground shooters. In Kunming some of the pilots used the "lake" for target practice.

November 11, 1941
Cool today. Two missions. Three of our ships fired on targets. Worked in the PM. A BT-9 and the Beechcraft arrived. Crew Chief Robert Smith restricted to base. [For being Absent Without Leave/AWOL, I believe]

November 12, 1941
Toungoo, Burma: Same old thing. Played ball with the staff—lost.

November 13, 1941
McMillan washed out ship #86. Ground looped it. Bob Neal had a wheel lock up. Got my pass for Rangoon. I damn near quit today. I was really angry.

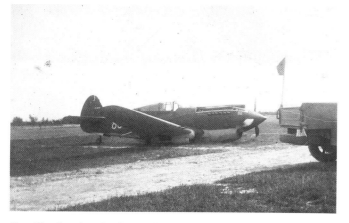

Even Vice Squadron Leaders washed them out (McMillan #86).

McMillan's #86.

I was angry because sometimes the work wasn't distributed fairly and, if you weren't buddies with the guy in charge, you got the "junk" work. As the youngest in the group I often got the "left-overs" and as a result, the work could be stressful.

A locked wheel could occur during a "hot" (fast) landing. Bob Neal may have "stood on the brakes" and heat friction may have seized the wheel. It took about 4 hours to replace the brake assembly.

November 14, 1941
Worked late. Tomorrow I get paid. My Rangoon pass starts tonight. We leave Toungoo at 7:30 PM and get into Rangoon 8:00 AM in the morning.

November 15, 1941
Regis, Jake (Frank Andersen), and I are staying at the Minto Mansions, 12 rupees a night. Went to the Shwe Dragon Pagoda built in 518 BC. Had to take

The Shwe Dragon Pagoda.

your shoes off when you went in it. Really made the rounds. Didn't get back to the hotel until 5 in the morning.

November 16, 1941
Feel rough as hell. I've got to go back (to Toungoo) on the 4 PM train. First time I danced with a girl since I left the States. It was OK.

November 17, 1941
Ship #11 caught fire at 1,000 feet up. The pilot landed in a rice paddy. The Colonel returned from Kunming. Some of us are going up this week. The ships must be set to go in 5 days.

We never found out why #11 caught fire. The pilot, Cross, was not injured.

November 18, 1941
Ship #87 washed out—"C" flight. That makes 7 damaged aircraft from our flight. $42,000 each.

It was late November or early December when some pilots came up with the idea to paint the famous sharks teeth on the P-40s. But it was Stan Regis who came up with the famous portraits of the devilish la

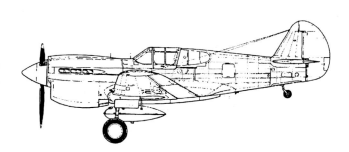

P-40—I was told a P-40 cost $42,000—Cheap.

dies that adorned the 3rd's aircraft. He told me he got the idea from a pin-up picture. Most of the ladies were done free hand without benefit of a stencil. As I recall it took him or his Chinese helpers about 1/2 hour to paint a lady. The ladies came in several poses. As I recall, the bodies were done in red with white wings.

The "Shark" motif may have been picked because Japan, as a fishing nation, was superstitious about sharks. But in China, many of the population had never seen a shark and believed the painted P-40 noses resembled 'tiger teeth.' To them a Flying Tiger, also

known as 'Fi Weung,' was a symbol of strength and vitality which the Chinese press used to describe the AVG successes.

The shark or tiger teeth.

The shark teeth.

The shark teeth. Rector's #36, Foshee and Mosse's #97. Who piloted #24?

Reed's devilish lady.

Regis standing beside another painted lady.

Criz admiring his lady.

Flight jackets were also decorated. My "lady" was done in red with some white highlights. Wish I still had it.

Stan Regis next to the famous "Tiger in the V" decal created by Henry Porter, a Disney artist.

November 19, 1941
A P-40 (Erik Shilling) and a Brewster had a dog-fight. The P-40 whipped hell out of it.

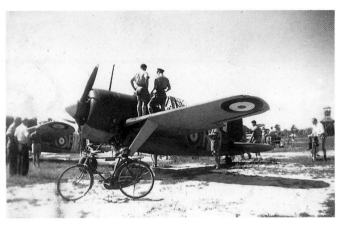

Brewster Buffalo.

The Brewster Buffalo was an aging British fighter/bomber built by the U.S. under British contract. The fighter was no match for "close quarters" fighting with the Japanese nor could it out dive the Japanese aircraft. In the coming air battles the Japanese soundly beat the Brewster, in part, because the Brits didn't use the "strike from above, hit and run" air tactics recommended by Chennault.

Robert Brouk standing in front of the radiator and lowered cooling flaps. Note also the guns.

November 20, 1941
Ship #8 burned a rod because an oil line failed. The 3rd's CO (Commanding Officer) went to Kunming this AM. Jean got married—too bad. She was Hazel's sister [my old West Palm Beach flame].

The Allison C-15 was "Prestone" cooled, similar to a typical automobile engine. During preflight we checked the radiator flaps, the coolant level and cooling lines. The cooling lines were labeled with white bands. The cooling liquid was a strong concentration of antifreeze (97 Ethylene Glycol) mixed with a little water. I didn't do much to the cooling system other than check the antifreeze level and the cooling lines. The Allison had a "coolant pump" but I never had to change one—only inspect it for leaks and tighten a single adjustment screw. We had no shortage of antifreeze, but we never threw any away. The "old" coolant could be recycled by "boiling" and filtering although we never did it. We changed the engine coolant every 50 hours. When I was in Kunming, I had one aircraft come back with most of the coolant gone. Engine vibration had cracked a cooling line. Fortunately, the engine didn't seize.

Burnt rods were often caused by an overheated engine brought on by the loss of engine coolant or low oil.

November 21, 1941
Toungoo, Burma: Three ships came back from Kunming. Got a letter from Ann and Johnnie (my sister and brother-in-law). Everything is OK in the States.

November 22, 1941
Got my first real scare today taxiing my ship. Damn near nosed it up.

Off-ground taxiing.

I was taxiing the aircraft somewhere. Guess I was in a hurry to get there, or felt the "need for speed." Anyhow I throttled the ship up and before I knew it, the tail was off the ground and the plane was going all over the field. Scared the hell out of me. It was the closest I'd ever come to flying a P-40. One heck of a thrill, but real scary. The CO would have wrung me out to dry had I wrecked that airplane. At the time, we didn't have many flyable aircraft. Shortly afterwards Chennault banned all off-ground tail taxiing. I never taxied the P-40 in a straight line because I couldn't see out the front. I always "S" turned the aircraft—taxied it left then right—until I reached my destination. I also taxied the aircraft with my head out of the cockpit to see where I was going.

November 24, 1941
Mondays are tough days, but this one went fast. "C" flight fired at the ground targets today.

November 25, 1941
Things are starting to click. It won't be long now before we go up the road.

November 26, 1941
I was all set to go up the road (to Kunming) when the CO put the screws to it. He said he needed me in Toungoo. Boy was I pi—ed off. The trip by convoy takes 15 days. We are now scheduled to leave by CNAC (air) next Saturday Dec 6. Ship #71 is running rough. Ships #85 and #88 are OK.

Taxiing the aircraft.

Pilots of the 3rd squadron.

November 23, 1941
Went to church. Biked to town, had waffles at Klines (a department store) in the PM.

Overend and Eric Shilling flew #71. Brouk and Greene flew #85. #85 was eventually shot down during the Rangoon air battle, December 23, 1941. Ken Jernstedt flew #88.

We all wanted to go to Kunming to cool weather and better living conditions.

#71's rough running engine could be caused by any of the following conditions in order of probability: 1) contaminated fuel (water), 2) cold engine, 3) carburetor heat or mixture, 4) excessively rich or lean mixtures, 5) insufficient fuel pressure, 6) prop out of track or balance, 7) excessive engine RPM, 8) defective spark plugs, 9) air leaks—backfire screens, 10) sticky valves.

The China National Aviation Corporation was jointly owned by the Chinese government and Pan American. The airline flew supplies from India to China, over some of the most treacherous terrain and weather on earth. Hump flying was very dangerous.

November 27, 1941
We played the pilots in baseball, for beer, and beat them 8 to 5. Col. Chennault pitched.

November 28, 1941
Didn't do much today. Had a hangover.

Left to right: VanTimmerman (Line Chief), Harvey Greenlaw (Staff), and Chennault (Group Commander).

November 29, 1941
Rumor has it we shove off Monday. Least that's what the CO (Olson) told us this afternoon. Boy that's good news. The guns were all loaded and oxygen was installed.

Ironic. We thought we were going north to Kunming. Little did we know, we'd be heading south to Rangoon.

Chennault's "strike from above" air tactics made oxygen necessary. The P-40 carried a small oxygen bottle stored in the baggage compartment behind the pilot's seat. I believe the oxygen supply lasted about 2 hours. We filled the portable bottles from large oxygen cylinders stored in the hangars. As far as I know all our aircraft were equipped with oxygen. The pilot's oxygen mask was one of the first issued by the Army Air Corps—a flimsy contraption. As I recall, oxygen equipment didn't require any special maintenance. We checked the oxygen gauge as part of our preflight.

November 30, 1941
Worked till 6:00 pm. Got all three aircraft in commission. Boy, if we don't leave, the boys will sure be unhappy.

December 1, 1941
Worked as usual. We have 23 ships ready to shove off. The Col. gave us a pep talk, so it looks like it will be soon.

Pep talk

As I recall, Chennault talked to us about the Japanese locations and warned us not to discuss operations with anyone because of Burmese spies. Some of the operations folks believed the Buddhist priests, the pongyis, spied for the Japanese. It was known that the Buddhists supported the Burmese independence movement. Some supporters of the movement disguised themselves as pongyis (Buddhist priests) and were known to have spied for the Japanese.

Pongyis—Buddhist priests.

December 2, 1941
23 more shopping days till Xmas, and still in Toungoo sweating it out.

December 3, 1941
Everything around here is "tomorrow." We're still here. Today 18 ships flew in formation. It's the most our squadron has put up yet, and they all came down (safely). Movie tonight is "Dance, Girl, Dance."

Flying formation.

December 4, 1941
Still here (in Toungoo). Put in for a Mandalay pass.

December 5, 1941
Pass approved. The CO canceled the move north till further notice. Left for Mandalay on the 9:20 PM train. Had plenty of can heating liquid (slang for beer and gin).

Mandalay race track. The race track was one of the finest I've ever seen. We stayed for 8 races. The track restaurant served great food.

Leper colony—what a lasting impression. Those people were bad off.

December 6, 1941

Arrived Mandalay at 7:00 am. Ate, got our room at the rest house. Went to the horse races at 2:00 pm, got back at 5:30 pm. Ate and left for Maymyo about 41 miles from Mandalay. Things didn't pan out there because of a total black out condition. Maymyo was a hill station, part of our early warning network.

December 7, 1941

Went to the St. Johns Leper Colony and really saw some bad cases, dying ones. Also went to the market. Went up Mandalay Hill. At 6:00 PM we left for Toungoo. Got home at 3:30 AM (morning).

Mandalay Hill, what a sight.

Chapter III
War Diary:
December 8, 1941-January 1, 1942

December 8, 1941
Got the news over the radio that the Japanese had bombed Pearl Harbor, Singapore, Manila, and Wake Island. The Colonel told us to get ready to move to Rangoon at 8:00 PM. The CO, Olson, went to Rangoon to get us a place to stay, but the Limeys [the British] wouldn't come across. So the move's canceled until tomorrow.

Yes, the December 8 date is correct. The Jaegersfontein crossed the International Date Line on the 26 of July and "gained a day." The dateline is in the Pacific, so at the time of the attack, it was December 7 in Hawaii, but December 8 in China.

What a surprise. We thought we were going to Kunming to fight for China. Now we were on our way to Rangoon, Burma. I don't believe we cared where we fought—Burma or China, it didn't matter. We were anxious to get going.

December 9, 1941
Still in Toungoo. The ships are flying patrol. Everyone is on alert. The Japanese really made it bad in Oahu. Many people killed or wounded. The President has declared war on Japan today. They won't last long now.

We were issued gas masks and helmets. On December 9th, the 3rd Pursuit had 28 pilots and 44 technicians and an unknown number of flyable aircraft.

December 10, 1941
The air raid alarm sounded at 3:20 AM. The alert ships took off. The rest of us got out of bed and got our ships running. A flight of Japanese bombers flew over and bombed Pegu about 30 miles south of us. I believe the bombs were really meant for us. Our ships didn't shoot any of the bombers, our boys lost them. One of our ships cracked up landing at night. P-40s don't have landing lights [This is incorrect, see below]. I go on alert duty at 6:00 PM tonight.

When the alarm sounded we bolted out of the beds and ran as fast as we could to our flight line. Adrenaline was pumping like crazy. When I reached my ships I immediately began the runups. In the distance I could hear the Japanese bombers. I was plenty scared and remember thinking "What's a falling bomb sound like?" "What do I do if one comes down? Jump in a trench?" The bombers missed us. Next day we learned they bombed Pegu.

Our fighters took off but lost the bombers. On the way back they faced a tricky night landing. The diary entry regarding landing lights is incorrect. The P-40 did have a small landing light in the wing, but we also used trucks, placed at the far ends of the runway, facing each other, to help night landings. The truck lights were turned and the landing field lit—at least part of it. Unfortunately Tex Hill landed long and cracked up. He survived.

December 11, 1941

Worked till 6:00 AM this morning (night shift—alert crew). I was supposed to have the rest of the day off, but was awakened at 11:00 AM. Told to pack up and get my truck loaded. The 3rd Squadron is going to Rangoon tomorrow at 4:00 AM (morning). Things really started popping here. The Japanese are only 60 miles from us in Thailand. I'm driving a 3 ton International.

I loaded up my 3 ton International truck with ammo, tires, wing jacks, hydraulic oil, tool boxes, and personal items. The training was finished and we were off to war.

We heard Thailand surrendered without firing a shot. Only sixty miles separated us from the Japanese but I never worried about it. It all seemed so surreal, as if we were making a movie. The notion of war hadn't settled in yet.

December 12, 1941

Started from Toungoo at 5:30 AM. Got to Rangoon at 12:30 PM. All the ships arrived. Mingaladon is the name of the aerodrome. It's a big place. CNAC is also here. The British have 12 Buffalos in the flying squadron. I'm very tired.

We were told that Rangoon was important to China. If Rangoon fell the Japanese could push all the way up to the Burma Road.

I left early in the morning because it was cooler and I wanted to avoid Japanese aircraft. Night travel was always safer. I packed everything because I didn't

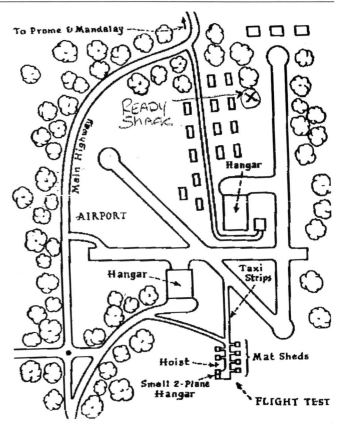

Mingaladon airfield. (Courtesy Eric Shilling from his book Destiny*)*

think I would return. Toungoo was a training facility and we were finished training.

Chennault told Olson he was on his own and set his headquarters up at Mingaladon. He was also to disperse his aircraft to nearby emergency fields. Olson was able to get us decent quarters and we ate well at the British mess. The Brits occupied one side of the field and we the other.

The ready shack—Mingaladon Aerodrome.

The pass was the principal means of identification. The Gurkas guards always compared the photo with the person. Handsome devil, wasn't I?

December 13, 1941
Picked up my pass today.

December 14, 1941
Quiet today. Got a pass to Rangoon, about 12 miles from the field. Had a few beers and a good time.

Rangoon was a frightened city. Everyone knew that invasion was imminent and the people were scared. The natives were in disarray. We did most of our drinking at the "Green Hotel." Years later, when I worked for Trans-Asiatic Airlines (TAA), I become best of friends with the owner's son, John Huie.

December 15, 1941
Had a big head all day. Worked the AM. Got the PM off. Got a nice set up in Rangoon. Mr. Minus sure is a nice fellow, as are his three daughters.

The Minus's were a friendly Anglo-Burmese family we visited when we went to the city. They made us feel at home. Stan and I were always welcome. After the Japanese invasion they went to India.

December 16, 1941
Worked all day. Hot. Lots of war talk.

December 17, 1941
We had the surprise of our lives this afternoon. A B-24 flew in with the Chief of the Air Corps (Asian Theater) General Brett. He's been touring this part of the world for a month. They aren't sure when they will leave. The Japanese have given us 72 hours to get out of Rangoon or we get bombed. 7 AM tomorrow is the deadline.

I was more impressed with Gen. Brett and the B-24 than the Japanese ultimatum. I didn't think much about it.

December 18, 1941
The ships patrolled all day. Nothing. Finished the book "What Makes Sammy Run"—very good. Sure would like to be home for Xmas.

Everyone was ready for war. Chennault moved the 1st and 2nd squadrons to Kunming, some 650 miles from Toungoo. While the 1st and the 2nd enjoyed the comforts of Chinese hospitality and cool weather, we were left sweltering in the Burmese heat and humidity. Even the Brits were issued gas masks, helmets, and tea cups.

December 19, 1941
Had another false alarm. I got my weekend leave. Went to Rangoon. Went to a show, then danced, then drank.

As I was dancing the Japanese were bombing Kunming.

December 20, 1941
Got reports from Kunming Station. Three Japanese bombers knocked down and 3 strafed bad by the 2nd squadron. Met a nice girl, June, an Anglo-Indian. Very smart. She's OK. Got blinded again.

I believe June was with the British USO. My drinking must have really impressed her. I don't recall going to any U.S. USO parties, although I do remember we had the American Red Cross in China.

December 21, 1941
One false alarm. I wanted to go to church but no transportation. First enemy action by the AVG in Kunming.

Transportation: Besides the bike, there was bus transportation.

The 1st and the 2nd Squadrons shot down the first enemy aircraft. Those of us in Rangoon felt the war had passed us by. Boy, were we in for a surprise.

December 22, 1941

Same old thing, one alarm. The weather is hot as hell. Wish we would move to Kunming soon. Rangoon is a good place to have a good time.

December 23, 1941

Got the hell bombed out of us for the first time. There were 75 bombers and a squadron of I-10 [Actually, they were probably Nates, KI-27s]. They bombed us at 10:30 AM. We lost Gilbert, so far Neil hasn't come back. Green bailed out and got strafed all the way down. Lucky no hits. Hayward's plane was all shot up. Lost three ships for sure. Jernstedt got one bomber. Rangoon really caught hell. Lots of dead both here and Rangoon.

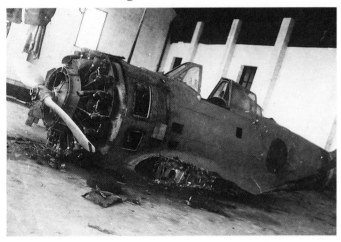

Downed Japanese aircraft.

We had little warning of the incoming Japanese aircraft. Suddenly bullets and bombs were hitting everywhere—the operations building, the hangar, the runway. Japanese aircraft strafed the few aircraft that were on the ground. Stan Regis and I jumped into the trench alongside our ready shack. During a pause in the bombing as we were trying to get off the airfield, Olson, the CO, drove by us in his jeep. He saw us but kept on going. Olson never mentioned the incident, nor did I, but I never forgot. Meanwhile the bombs kept coming. Finally, after what appeared to be an eternity of shelling and strafing, a British chap in a lorry stopped and picked us up. Minutes later we were

off the field. Five miles away Japanese bombs were blowing up the Rangoon docks. There was a lot of black smoke coming from the dockyards. It was impressive. Twenty minutes later a second wave of bombers arrived. Neil Martin's Tomahawk was shot down. He was our first AVGer to die in battle. Gilbert was next. His plane caught fire and crashed. Green was also shot up but bailed out and landed safely. On his way down a British pilot fended off some Japanese pilots who were strafing him. I saw him in his parachute. When the all clear sounded Stan and I started back towards the airfield. We came across a British lad with half his "buttocks" blown away. We stopped the bleeding and packed the half naked boy into a nearby lorry and drove him to the British hospital. I was there when they fixed him up but I never saw him again. After the battle the 3rd Squadron claimed 6 confirmed victories, the British claimed 7! Our search parties found 32 other Japanese aircraft. Later I learned that 54 Japanese bombers left Bangkok. They picked up a fighter escort near Burma. The 74 planes split into two groups, one for Rangoon and the other for my airfield at Mingaladon. My squadron (3rd Pursuit) sent up 14 aircraft. I don't recall how many aircraft the British sent up.

That evening I went into the city for a few beers and a look around. The place was a mess, filled with people running in every direction with the few belongings they owned. The city had an odd smell.

The same day three AVG pilots ferrying Curtiss CW-21 Demon fighters from Rangoon to Kunming

Lacy Mangleburg

crash landed in the mountains about 60 miles from Kunming. Two pilots, Shilling and Merritt, survived but Lacy Mangleburg died in the crash. For unknown reasons, all mention of the accidents and Mangleburg's death were withheld from "official" AVG records until January 9, 1942.

Lacy was from Georgia, always singing "Georgia On My Mind." He was a happy-go-lucky chap. He always had a good word for the ground crew.

(L-R) Ken Jernstedt, Tom Haywood, Chuck Older, R.T. Smith

I also crewed #8181 (#88) for Ken Jernstedt, a likeable chap, and a friend to boot. Ken is a soft spoken person who could fly an airplane. Back in 1981 he sent me a note. "I know I've said it to you before—many thanks for your fine work on "88." It's more sincere now than it would have been 40 years ago because of the enclosed card." /s/ Ken Jernstedt. The card was a picture of himself, Gen, his wife, and the family. I kept the letter.

December 24, 1941

700 dead in Rangoon, 12 dead here. 30 hurt. More expected tomorrow. Never thought I would spend Christmas Eve on a boat in Rangoon. I went to town and met some Americans. They took me aboard. They really had some good coffee and eats. Rangoon is like a ghost town and it smells like a funeral.

Regis and I went aboard an American cargo ship. The captain gave us cigarettes, candy bars, and anything we wanted. I believe the ship was sunk at the dock the next day.

December 25, 1941

We really got a present from the Japanese. They came over again and neatly dropped their eggs [bombs]. All the P-40s and Brewsters got off. They shot down 27 enemy aircraft. Boy, are we playing for keeps now. Gen. Wavell, the ranking Allied commander in the theater [China, Burma, India], was near my slit trench.

Rangoon victories.

We were much better prepared for the Japanese. The early warning net gave us plenty of time to get the aircraft off. The enemy bombers dropped most of their bombs on the south east part of the field. The barracks were hit. What a heck of a way to spend Christmas.

Rangoon victories.

The Rangoon air victories were the only cheerful news. The Allies had taken a beating in the Philippines, Battan, Hong Kong, and Pearl Harbor. Hong Kong fell on Christmas Day.

The shell hole was the equivalent of a "fox" hole. It was a slit trench about 3' wide and 5' deep. It offered some protection from bombs and direct strafing. I don't recall talking with Gen. Wavell either be-

Rangoon damage—British aircraft.

The slit trench—bomb shelter—shell hole.

fore or after the Japanese attack, but I believe he was as scared as I was.

December 26, 1941
A false alarm about 10:30 AM. All's well. Worked on the ships.

After the raids there were lots of repair work. I fixed a bullet hole shot through an elevator. Took a

piece of 2" wide fabric tape. Cut a piece about 2' long then tucked the fabric under the leading edge of the stabilizer and pulled it tight over the upper part of the elevator. Next I doped the fabric. The hot climate quickly dried the dope. Two more coats of dope finished the job. Bob Neal and Frank Andersen tell about their fixit experiences: "The bullet was shot through the metal leading edge. The ground crew took a hammer and peened the jagged metal edges back into the hole. Next they took some fabric tape, placed it on the leading edge, and pulled it forward for a snug fit. Last they doped it several times. The fix was as good as new." Frank Andersen also recalls, "Bob Neal came back from a raid with his rudder fabric blown away. I got some replacement fabric. wrapped it around the rudder several times, doped it up good and let it dry. The fix worked."

Japanese aircraft dropped leaflets on Rangoon. The leaflets said paratroopers would be landing soon. I believe if paratroopers had landed we would have gone to China.

December 27, 1941
At 10:30 the 2nd Squadron came down from Kunming to relieve us. But at 11:00 AM they took off for Toungoo. The whole works is screwed up, so here we sit in Rangoon. We have 47 Japanese aircraft to our credit.

With the war going so well, I didn't want to leave Rangoon. Spirits were high. We were whipping the hell out of the Japanese and we felt invincible, but the Japanese had invaded Burma and it was clear we had to move or be captured.

December 28, 1941
After the 2nd squadron arrived at Toungoo they were told to go back to Rangoon. We are to take off for Toungoo at 3:00 PM, then by CNAC to Kunming. We arrived at Toungoo at 8:30 PM. Next they flew us to Lashio. Arrived at 11:00 PM. We slept in Lashio because we couldn't get radio contact to Kunming. Slept in the hostel. Boy was it cold. I damn near froze to death.

December 29, 1941
Arrived Kunming at 9:30 AM. Regis and I have a

room all to ourselves, hot water, good eats. Everything is perfect here. Cold all day long, just like our fall weather back in Michigan. American cigarettes, candy bars, nuts, V.O., 5 Crown [whiskey] etc.

Kunming was a "warm springs," a nice place to relax. After living in tropics for 6 1/2 months Kunming was a blessed relief. The temperature and humidity was much lower, and there were no bugs.

Kunming.

Kunming is situated at the north end of a huge muddy lake about 6,000 feet above sea level. The airfield was located 3 miles from the old walled city. Kunming was much cleaner then Rangoon or Toungoo. There were no beggars. The old city had charm. Although the city had been a Japanese target for several years, I saw little bomb damage. Outside

Kunming gates—entrance to the city.

December 30, 1941
Don't have to work until tomorrow. The city is large and has many people. The food is good. It was also a place where you could change money.

R&R at the warm springs.

The field with aircraft.

The airfield.

December 31, 1941
Both of my ships came in today. Took them to the woods for an inspection. The field altitude is 6,047', and you can tell it.

The Chinese had some strange customs, like binding women's feet. I felt sorry for the girls.

The airfield was huge compared to Toungoo. Revetments surrounded buildings and offered some protection against bombs. After I arrived, hundreds of Chinese coolies began building a thick stone runway for the heavy B-29 bombers. Coolies were still working on the runway when we left. Our fighters used the adjacent grass strips.

The field was located at 6,000 feet and the engines often backfired because the altitude affected the fuel mixture. Backfiring got so bad we pulled the backfire screens out of the engine. The fix smoothed out the engines but created a real fire hazard. When a C15 engine backfires it "explodes"—which is very scary and definitely not good for the engine. Pilots would accidentally backfire the engine if they pulled the throttle back quickly.

On start-up we "cracked the throttle" a bit more, and worried about over priming the engine. We also pumped the wobble pump a bit more to keep the fuel pressure up (altitude affects fuel pressure). I don't remember making any carburetor adjustments to compensate for the field elevation.

Airfield construction.

The field was guarded by Chinese soldiers.

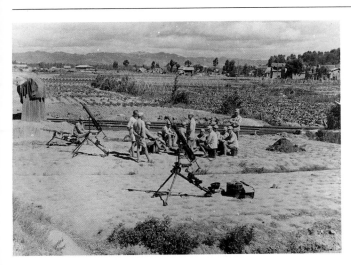

Guarding the field.

January 1, 1942
Worked all day. Will have ship #71 out tomorrow. The money exchange is $5 Chinese to $1 US. It was very cold today—45 degrees. A little rain.

I hadn't planned well for the cold weather. We were issued gloves, jackets, and caps. I bought a pair of long johns. The gear was quite comfortable.

Cold weather uniforms—(L-R) Chuck Older, Duke Hedman, Bill Reed, Joe Poshefko.

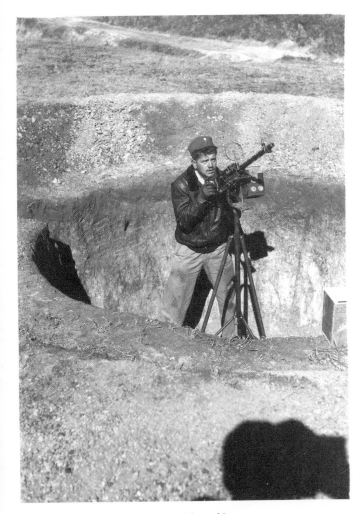

Airfield protection—Jake Andersen with machine gun.

Chapter IV
War Notes: January 2–July 4, 1942

The following "war notes" are my recollections of events that took place between January 2 and July 4, 1942. They are based on memory joggers from Dan Hoyle's official 3rd Pursuit Squadron AVG diary, R.T. Smith's (AVG pilot) *Tale of a Tiger*, and Erik Shillling's (AVG pilot) *Destiny*.

January 2-3, 1942
"Cloudy," Marion Baugh, a flight instructor, was killed in his Ryan trainer on a routine training flight. Julian Terry, an administration clerk, was injured in a freak aircraft accident. Crew Chief Seiple arrived from Toungoo at 5:00 pm.

January 4, 1942
I was released from temporary duty with the 2nd squadron and joined up with the 3rd. Personnel were upset about the possibility of joining the Army.

As early as January, the Army pressured us to re-enlist. We were told that if we remained overseas after July 4th, we would be subject to the Chinese draft rules. Some personnel tendered their resignations, but the resignations were refused.

January 5-6, 1942
Continued alert duty by our pilots and crew chiefs at night.

January 7, 1942
Crew Chief Gallagher assigned to our Squadron. Ken Jernstedt was appointed Transportation Officer.

January 8, 1942
Continued alert duty. Lacy Mangleburg was killed in an airplane crash while en route from Lashio to Kunming [see December 23, 1941]. Merritt killed in a car at Mingaladon Rangoon during a dusk landing.

Merritt was sleeping in a parked car next to one of the trucks we used to light the field. One of our ships returning late from a raid landed long and hit Merritt's car.

January 9-11, 1942
All night and day alert duty for pilots and technicians. Marion Baugh's funeral. Charlie Mott shot down and believed captured by the Japanese.

Charlie Mott is believed to be the first American prisoner of war taken in air combat by the Japanese. The Japanese had several status levels of "prisoners of war." Charlie was given a "high level" POW status. Unfortunately that status didn't keep him off the "River Kwai" railroad project. Once the war ended, Charlie waited a month in Calcutta trying to get transportation home. The Air Transportation Command, the Army, and the Navy all classified him as a "civilian" and refused help.

January 12, 1942
Radio man Harvey Cross went to Paoshan, China for duty. There was a photography mission to Loakai,

Hagiang, China, to photograph military objectives and troop concentrations.

Eric Shilling recalls just a single photo ship. One of the mechanics from the 2nd modified #53 for photo reconnaissance. Later he believes they converted #53 back to a fighter and changed the number to #22. As I recall the camera was mounted in the baggage compartment. After the aircraft completed a mission, the photographers removed the film, developed it, and sent the pictures to Headquarters. Joe Pietsker and James Regis were our photographers. I never directly worked with the photo equipment. The photo missions were often deep into enemy territory and I'm sure the possibility of engine failure and capture was a concern.

January 13, 1942
Routine alert duty. Dupouy and Shilling and Haywood on a photo mission. Bombers sighted over Mengtsz 128 miles from Kunming.

Mengtsz was a remote airfield located near the Indochina border. The Chinese had a couple of old Russian fighters up there but they couldn't do much against the Japanese aircraft. The field was primarily used as a refueling stop for aircraft going or coming from Hanoi and other parts of Indochina. Aircraft returning from a mission were given about 80 gallons of gas, just enough to get them back to Kunming. Frank Andersen, one of the crew chiefs, tells the story about pilots waiting to get fueled up. "Seems it took almost an hour to pump 80 gallons of gas into the aircraft. The pilots were nervous because they were close to enemy airfields and sitting P-40s made great targets. The folks in Mengtsz couldn't figure out why the Studerbaker fueling trucks were taking so long to pump fuel, so Group asked Frank Metasavage and myself to go up and fix the problem. It turned out to be clogged fuel screens. No one bothered to tell the Chinese about the screens. Frank and I cleaned them and in a matter of hours we were back in full production."

Mengtsz wasn't a particularly nice location but was better than many of the places I stayed. The AVG also had a radio/warning station there.

Russian fighter flown by Chinese pilots. Probably a Polikarpov I-15.

January 14-15, 1942
Routine training. Squadron went on a secret mission. R.T. Smith promoted to Flight Leader. Shilling appointed Group Photography Officer. Gunvordahl (pilot) resigned from the AVG.

Mostly photographic missions. The missions were conducted when the remote stations reported enemy movement.

R.T. Smith was a super pilot with 9 victories. R.T. wrote *Tale of A Tiger*, an excellent book based upon his war diary. R.T. passed away three days after he reviewed our book draft. He shares his comments with us in Chapter 7. He will be missed.

At this time, Stubbs, Fuller, Knapp, Houle, Bernsdorf (all pilots) and five ground crew resigned from the AVG for various reasons.

January 16, 1942
Dupouy and Shilling returned from Mengtsz—a secret mission. First air raid alarm sounded in Kunming. No action.

Besides the traditional wailing sirens, the Chinese used a visual system to warn the population of a pending air raid. Throughout the city they hoisted large colored balls up flag poles. Two red balls signaled imminent air raid. One red ball signaled warning—enemy aircraft sighted. One green ball—all clear.

January 17, 1942
Haywood, Older, Shilling, and McMillan engaged three bombers, shot two down and forced the other down. All pilots returned. McMillan's plane had a bullet hole in the wing length wise. The tip was easily replaced. The squadron left on a photo mission to Hanoi. Hanoi is one of the largest Japanese airfields in French Indochina.

The late model P-40s were equipped with 52 gallon drop tanks used to extend the range of the aircraft. The tanks were used on the Indochina photo missions. The tanks were not difficult to mount.

January 18, 1942
Mott (2nd squadron) confirmed shot down and captured by the Japanese.

January 19, 1942
Routine. We have an old Russian bomber on the field being tried out for different purposes.

January 20, 1942
Prepared for an air raid. Swindle dropped from the rolls of the AVG because he failed to return from a 60 day leave.

Getting ready for an air raid usually meant "scrambling" the aircraft and figuring out how to survive the incoming air attack. The slit trenches were popular survival locations, but so were the woods.

Swindle left for the States the 18th of October. He didn't come back.

Swindle.

Aircraft scramble.

January 21, 1942
The Chinese aircraft factory near the airfield is doing a good job repairing damaged aircraft.

Chinese mechanics.

The Chinese mechanics were super technicians, most knew their jobs, were hard working, and did lots of tedious maintenance work. Most were trained at the CAMCO factory. I worked with Chun Gee, Pak Lee, George Lum, Kee Pon, George Shee, Lem Wu, and Francis Yee. After the war, several went to work for the "Flying Tiger Lines."

January 22, 1942
10 Russian bombers, flown by Chinese pilots and accompanied by 1st Pursuit fighters attacked Hanoi. Bombs missed their primary target but succeeded in bombing Haiphong. Japanese anti-aircraft shot down one bomber. The other bombers returned to Changyi. The 3rd Pursuit sent 6 planes to Mengtsz to protect the returning bombers.

January 23-24, 1942
Routine, Eight 3rd Pursuit aircraft escorted 18 Chinese bombers to Hanoi.

January 25, 1942
The 1st Pursuit left today to support the 2nd Pursuit stationed Mingaladon, Rangoon, Burma.

January 26, 1942
Continued alert all day. Chungking 280 miles east of Kunming was bombed.

January 27, 1942
We had our squadron picture taken today. All present except Crew Chief Olson who was in Calcutta selling film footage of the Rangoon air battle.

Notice the 5 dogs in the squadron picture. None survived. The Chinese considered dogs a delicacy. In China the natives ate monkeys and dogs. They fattened them up and ate them. I don't recall ever knowingly eating dog or monkey meat, although others told me it was quite tasty. Morgan Vaux recalls a different experience. "A few months after I arrived at my radio outpost, the Chinese soldiers threw a party. What ap-

"Hell's Angels" mechanics.

peared to be chicken legs were served. Days later I noticed several puppies missing at the Pagoda, then I remembered how small the chicken legs were and how sweet they tasted. I decided not to ask about the puppies."

Olson, one of our ground crew, had taken some movies of the Rangoon air action and at the time was selling the footage to one of the news organizations.

January 28-30, 1942
Continued alert duty. The Japanese were cutting in on our radio frequency and making it hard to hear.

The Japanese knew our frequencies but there was no direct Japanese attempt to jam the frequencies. On occasions, however, Japanese speaking fluent English would try to misdirect our pilots.

January 31, 1942
Continued alert. Our pilots were presented with Chinese pilot wings.

February 1-2, 1942
Continued alert. Gallagher and Osborne left for Mengtsz. Chinese Minister of Justice, Chu Chen, was briefed in the Chinese hangar and asked about welfare and morale of the AVG. Gen. Chennault was present at the ceremonies. The pilots were given bed coverings of silk. The Chinese band played both countries national anthems.

Chennault had a serious morale problem. Folks were unhappy. The ground crew felt the pilots were getting all the glory and awards. No decorations for us, no silk bed coverings, and little press coverage. Besides, the Army was pressuring us to reenlist. The pilots weren't happy either. They were ordered to strafe heavily protected low level targets—risky business.

Story goes that one of our ground crew left a live-in Chinese prostitute at Mengtsz for the relief crew. I understand she was quite skilled. I'd write more, but can't afford to break up marriages at this late date.

February 4, 1942
Routine flying and training. Another photo mission. Continued alert. McMillan assumed command of the

squadron in Olson's absence. Olson went to Chungking for a meeting.

McMillan was a likable, easy going, chap. Just one heck of a nice fellow, a good commander and pilot.

Routine flying and training.

February 5, 1942
Our pilots were ordered to check out Chinese pilots in our P-40s. Not too happy about the situation. We showed the Chinese pilots how to taxi the aircraft.

I don't believe the Chinese pilots were any rougher on the ships than our own pilots.

February 6, 1942
Continued alert duty. Four Chinese pilots made successful take offs and landings. One Chinese pilot ground looped the P-40. No news from Rangoon or Toungoo about the movement of the squadrons.

The Japanese ground forces in Burma were advancing on Mandalay. The 1st and 2nd squadrons were set to leave Rangoon. On February 6th the 1st pursuit shot down seven Japanese fighters, the RAF shot down 3. Chennault cabled Newkirk, the 2nd's Commander, and suggested "the allies deny the Japs use of the roads for movement of supplies east of Moulmein."

The British abandoned massive amounts of war material. In some places the stuff was piled 40-50' high. After the British left Rangoon, Frank Andersen went into the city to get a couple of trucks. "The trucks were loaded with ammunition. We backed them up to the docks and dumped the whole load then drove them back to Mingaladon. We didn't stay in Rangoon too long after that because the Japanese were coming up from Moulmein. Just before we left Rangoon, we ran low on P-40 ammo so Frank Metasavage and I took a jeep up to Toungoo to get some more. We found a loaded ammunition truck and started back to Rangoon. We got a ways down the road and the truck ran out of gas so we pushed it with the jeep most of the way back to Rangoon. As we neared Rangoon you could hear gunfire. I don't know who was doing the fighting because the British were long gone. It may have been the Gurkas, it certainly wasn't the Burmese. When the British declared Rangoon an open city most of the Indian merchants left. The only ones left were Burmese—not much."

February 7, 1942
Chinese pilots continuing to be checked out in our P-40s. Sandell was killed in Rangoon. His airplane went into spin while testing, the one that was shot up by the Japanese in the last raid on Mingaladon. The tail section was believed to have been the problem.

February 8, 1942
Crew Chief Olson returned from Calcutta. He sold some film footage of the AVG Rangoon action to a news group.

February 9, 1942
Continued alert. Seven more Chinese pilots checked out in our P-40s.

The Japanese were advancing on Rangoon. The Allies were retreating. I believe it was in Mandalay that Doc Segrave gave Regis and myself his car. We were in Kunming, so we asked one of the ground crew to drive it up the road for us. The car eventually showed up in Kunming. Frank Andersen, however, was still in Rangoon. "You could see the bombs coming down, but they didn't look like bombs. They looked like someone dumping a bucket of silver leaves out the door. You could see them flash as they came out of the aircraft. When the Japanese bombed us at night, they came in with their running lights on. They'd

come over the field, drop some bombs, make a "U" turn come back over the top of us and drop more bombs. The Japanese were good. They never missed the runway.

Once we couldn't use the east west runway because of a couple of unexploded bombs. So what do you do? We got some Burmese out there and they packed dirt on top of them. The bombs didn't go off so we left them there. Course we didn't stay there too much longer. On the way out of Rangoon we liberated a liquor store—took case loads of Scotch and loaded it on the jeep. When we got to Magwe we bribed an air crew to fly a Burmese family to India. The bribe cost us a couple cases of Scotch. We also liberated a truck, gassed it up and helped another Burmese family escape."

February 10-11, 1942
Pilots and technicians from the 2nd Pursuit arrived Kunming from Mingaladon via Toungoo and Lashio. Most of the AVG had left Rangoon.

The 2nd Pursuit Squadron "Panda Bear" aircraft.

February 12, 1942
Paul Green and Parachute rigger Hooker went up in a BT-9. At 11,000 feet Hooker jumped out of the aircraft to test the parachute. He made a safe landing. This type of jumping didn't happen often.

Criz strapping on his parachute.

February 13, 1942
Green made an altitude test with a funnel like apparatus attached to the air cooler. He had engine trouble so landed. The apparatus served as a crude "supercharger."

February 14-18, 1942
Singapore surrendered on the 15th. Continued alert duty. Pilots received 5th class medals for their performance against the Japanese. Japanese will put full attention on Rangoon. The Award Ceremony was strictly a pilot's affair. No medals for the ground crew.

February 19, 1942
Crew Chief Rogers was transferred from Headquarters Engineering to our squadron. Some Japanese cross the Salween River.

February 20, 1942
Christensen and Hoffman flew to Chang-yi to look at some bombs for the P-40s. They returned to Kunming.

February 21, 1942
Hoffman and Riffer left by car for Chang-yi to get some bombs.

February 22, 1942
Continued alert. Maymyo and Mandalay were bombed today.

February 23, 1942
Rangoon has been evacuated. Supplies are being given away to the AVG and RAF. The AVG are out of Mingaladon airfield (Rangoon). The docks, buildings and airfield are being mined. Pilots Olson, Jernstedt, Reed and Hedman went on a photographic mission. Reed and Hedman became separated and were lost somewhere near Mileh, China.

P-40s on the line.

February 24, 1942
Olson attempted to locate Hedman and Reed. He failed to locate them. It is assumed they are all right. Crew Chiefs Schramm and Stiple left for Mileh, China, to fix Reed and Hedman's planes.

February 25-27, 1942
Stan and I were ordered to relieve Osborne and Gallagher in Mengtsz. It takes 3 days to reach Mengtsz by truck.

When I got to Mengtsz, Osborne asked me for the Kunming exchange rate. I didn't know what the exact rate was and gave him some off the wall number-much lower then the prevailing rate. Boy, was he angry when he discovered the actual rate. Seems he lost some money on an exchange. I suppose I owe him. Should we meet again, he gets a free book and a meal at any of our Columbus, Georgia restaurants.

While I was in Mengtsz, Regis went to the Mogo mines to buy some "black market" pewter. I believe the mines were in Indochina (strictly off-limits) and were run by the French. Young children were used to haul the ore out of the mines in small bags.

February 28-March 4, 1942
Routine duties.

One of the lasting impressions I had of China was an incident that took place near Mengtsz. Two Chinese soldiers had stolen some goods. They were marched to the center of a circle surrounded by other soldiers and beaten with large thick sticks until their arms and hands were quite broken. Even after the thieves fell down, the soldiers continued to beat them until they were unconscious. The beatings impressed me. Thievery wasn't tolerated in the Chinese Army. Begging wasn't tolerated either, although I'd see an occasional beggar .

March 5-8, 1942
We are relieved. "Pappy" Boyington's flight crash lands in Wenshan, China (March 5).

When Stan and I returned to Kunming, we were told the 2nd Squadron had lost 4 aircraft near Wenshan near the Indochina border. All had crash landed in a

A beggar.

rice paddy. The aircraft were escorting President Chiang and his wife, the Madam, up to Chungking. About half way up the flight leader, Boyington, turned the flight back because of low fuel and bad weather. Unfortunately the P-40s ran out of gas and crash landed just a few miles from the Japanese. The pilots survived, but the "old man" (Chennault) was plenty steamed over loosing the four ships. As I recall our Line Chief asked Regis, myself, and Major Chen, a Chinese interpreter, to salvage the ships before the natives cut the remains up for pots and pans. We checked out a 6X6 flatbed truck, a jeep, tools, some spare props, and some other assorted parts taken from the "graveyard." Before we left Kunming I bought a case of Dry Sack sherry loaded it into the truck, drove the truck onto a railroad flatcar, and rode it all the way to Mengtsz. When we arrived we were quite snockered and burnt all over from the locomotive coal sparks. I honestly don't know how we drove the truck off the flatcar. The Chinese escorted us the rest of the way to the crash site.

March 9-10, 1942
En route to Wenshan, China.

En route to Wenshan we stopped at a small village for the night. The village was run by a local war lord who invited us to spend the night with him. In one of the rooms was an old Chinese man close to death. Next to him was a casket, a lit candle, and a small bowl with an egg on top of some rice. I later learned the egg symbolized rebirth in the Hindu religion. One of the family members asked if I had some medicine. I gave them a couple aspirin which they gave the old man. Apparently the aspirin helped; he was still alive the next day.

Morgan Vaux recalls; "On the way to Iliang, I saw several dead Chinese beside the road, the result of a Japanese air raid. Mr. Sun, my interpreter, said the bodies would remain there, by custom, until someone claimed them." "Also I saw an infant wrapped up like a mummy, tied high up in a tree. Mr. Sun explained that the infant was probably deformed or incurably ill and was left to die. Such was the local peasant custom."

A cemetery.

March 11, 1942
We arrive at the wreck scene.

By the time we arrived at the crash site, the coolies had pulled the aircraft out of the muck. It was a wonder the pilots survived. A true testimonial to their piloting skills and the P-40 construction. The C model was built in two pieces and joined at the centerline. The joint where the two wing sections connected acted as a skid in case of a "belly" landing. Two aircraft were wrecked beyond repair. The props were smashed and the wings badly damaged. The other two ships were flyable but needed lots of repair. The landing gear was a mess, the props were bent, and the hydraulics were questionable. We replaced the props with spares and fixed the landing gear as best we could. Next we cut a narrow take-off strip right through a cemetery, by a rice paddy, down an embankment, and off the end of a cliff. The Chinese built the strip in two days. The strip was just long enough to get a "light" P-40 off. We removed the pilot's armor plate and most of the gas.

March 16, 1942
The salvaged aircraft fly.

On or around March 15 Boyington arrived. I'm not sure why he volunteered to fly the aircraft out. We could have easily "hauled" them back to Kunming. I do know Chennault was plenty steamed about losing 4 aircraft. As Boyington puts it in his book *Baa Baa Black Sheep*, after he crashed the aircraft he returned to a "cold" Kunming reception. *"I volunteered to fly them out if we could get them fixed."*

We put 30 gallons of gas into the tank, barely enough to get him home. I was sure the aircraft would fly, but had no idea if the brakes or landing gear would work and at the time I didn't have the equipment to do the checks. I told Boyington he was going to have to put the coals to it and fly it "gear down" all the way. I just didn't trust the hydraulics. We moved the aircraft to the absolute end of the strip. Pappy started the engine, barely warmed it up, and pushed it full throttle. He had the engine screaming. *"Pushed the throttle forward till the manifold pressure was well into the red. Plane flew nose high for a mile till it leveled out."* I remember he was barely flying when he hit the end of the strip. The rest of his trip was uneventful. I marvel how he flew those aircraft off that mountain strip. Greg left the AVG soon after he salvaged the two aircraft.

March 21, 1942
Crew Chief Johnny Fauth died in a Japanese air raid on Magwe, Burma. Pilots Jernstedt and Dupouy were injured. Olson and Hedman arrived at the airfield after the raid.

Frank Andersen recalls, "Group sent us to Magwe for awhile. It was in Magwe that the Japanese hit us and we lost crew chief, Johnny Fauth. At the time I was in the barracks and I could hear the Japanese aircraft making a pass over the runway—firing all the time. I didn't know what to do so I dove out the window and ran for the bush."

Johnny was hit in the shoulder by a Japanese bullet after he and another crew chief had freed a Hurricane pilot from his burning aircraft. He was running for cover when shrapnel tore into his jaw, one eye, and blew most of his arm off. Johnny was the only AVG crew chief killed in action.

March 22, 1942
Japanese had bombed Magwe again. All but 6 Hurricanes and 4 P-40s were damaged beyond repair. Wenshan is a much less dangerous place to be then Magwe.

March 23, 1942
The 3rd Pursuit was evacuating Magwe, Burma. The Japanese bombing had taken it's toll. Chennault sent the 3rd north to Loiwing, China.

March 28, 1942
Boyington arrives at Loiwing. He will arrive Wenshan soon to fly the second aircraft out.

MacArthur arrived briefly in Australia after his escape from the Philippines.

April 1, 1942
Boyington flies to Wenshan.

Pappy stayed in Kunming a day before returning to pick up the second ship. That night we tipped a couple glasses of rice wine. Pleasant stuff.

April 2-3, 1942
Boyington flies the second aircraft back to Mengtsz. We prepared the second ship much as the first. The second ship also had an uneventful trip back.

April 4-15, 1942
Salvage activity continues on the other downed aircraft.

We took the guns out of the unsalvageable aircraft, pulled out what we could from the wrecked bodies and took the damaged wing off. The P-40 wing came in one piece. It was held on by 12 large bolts. Next the coolie labor lifted the aircraft two feet off the ground, by hand, and pushed a skid under it—amazing. The coolies had to pull the skid a couple hundred yards to the truck. Next we hoisted the skid onto the flatbed truck and drove it to the waiting train

to Mengtsz. We repeated the process for the other aircraft. Truck, fuselages, and wings were loaded on the flatcars for the trip back to Kunming.

Bataan surrenders to the Japanese April 9, 1942.

April 13, 1942
Regis and Chen go to Indochina.

Around April 13th our interpreter Major Chen suggested a side trip into Lao Cai, Japanese occupied Indochina. He knew where to get cases of cheap French Cotab cigarettes. The idea was to take them back to Kunming and put them to work on the black market. I decided against the trip, but Regis and the Major went. They bought back lots of cigarettes which later turned a handsome profit. Had the Japanese caught them they would have been shot as spies. Black market activity was part of the Chinese and AVG culture, and the risks were great but so were the rewards. On one occasion I did a deal involving a couple of gallons of pills, making a few dollars. I also exchanged money—for profit. As a soldier, war profiteering didn't seem all that bad in China. After all, we were risking our lives in support of national objectives. I was lucky with my profiteering, some AVGers weren't. Frank Andersen recalls, "Frank Metasavage, my roommate, and I had just returned from the field and found our bunk area ransacked. We asked the house boy who did it. He said some guy from HQ looking for stuff. Frank was angry. He went over to HQ, got into an argument with Skip Adair, Chennault's recruiter, and punched him out. Frank left the outfit the next day and was shortly discharged."

A Chinese village.

"I've tried several times to get him reinstated (in the AVG) but no luck. Frank was a good mild manner fellow who served honorably. I believe he was discharged under extenuating circumstances and our current AVG leadership should reconsider reinstatement."

April 14, 1942
As I recall, we took the train from Wenshan to Kunming. The journey was uneventful. Some beautiful countryside.

April 15, 1942
The 3rd Squadron decided they needed some of us in Kunming so Regis and I stayed. The rest of the squadron went to Loiwing.

April 16, 1942
Had to take a load of bombs from Kunming to Paoshan. Delivered the bombs and returned to Kunming. Seems like we are always on some special mission.

The most frightening experience I had was when Regis and I were ordered to take a truck load of bombs

Burma road.

Chinese retreat on the Burma Road.

from Kunming to Paoshan some 200 miles down the Burma Road. Paoshan was one of our outlying air bases and was a popular "bomb-loading" and refueling stop for our pilots going to Burma. We had just entered one of the gorges on the Burma Road and were traveling up a steep grade. As we made a sharp turn around a bend, a group of armed Chinese soldiers,

deserters most likely, stopped us. They wanted the truck but we weren't about to give it up. They threatened to shoot us. We tried to reason with them for what seemed an eternity in our pidgin Chinese. The standoff ended when we sprayed the road with our Tommy guns. The soldiers let us go. It never occurred to me as we were driving away that a couple well placed bullets into our bomb load could have made for a very unpleasant day. Stan and I were so scared we shot our tommy guns at every bend in the Burma Road—all the way down to Paoshan—nervous energy I suppose.

April 18, 1942
US bombers bombed Tokyo and Yokohama Japan. Radioman Cross left for Wenshan, Burma, to set up a radio station. He took a load of bombs with him. Radioman Lussier of Group joined the radio station contingent here. Crew Chiefs Rogers and Olson also

left for Wenshan to service aircraft. Six Army transports arrived from Calcutta, India. Pilot Prescott, attached to us, shot down a Japanese observation plane.

The AVG had eight 400 watt twin channel transmitter stations scattered throughout China. The ground stations were outstanding, the stuff in our ships, less so. Rich Richardson, one of our radio men, recalls "Parts of the ground equipment were hand made by the Chinese, including the nuts and bolts!—Amazing. Resistors were hand made in molds."

Radio station.

We knew the Japanese monitored our frequencies and on several occasions our radio operators vectored Japanese pilots away from our unprotected fields by pretending to talk to our "phantom" pilots.

Morgan Vaux recalls, "Soon after I arrived in Kunming, I was reassigned as a station master near a small village called Iliang. Iliang was southeast of Kunming and served as part of our early warning air raid network. I was assigned an interpreter, Mr. Sun and a Chinese cook. Before I left for Iliang, Mr. Sun and I picked up a Chinese 60 watt transmitter and an RCA commercial receiver at the Chinese radio factory called the 'Black Dragon Pool'. On the way to the station I decided to tune the transmitter but overlooked the grounding. The transmitter shocked me so bad I almost fell off the truck. After we reached our destination, I set the radio station up in a small pagoda. The roof was the traditional sway-back style made of tile and open in the in the center. On the op-

posite side of the entrance was a large Buddha. The transmitter and receiver shared the platform with the Buddha. I strung the antenna from one pointed roof tile over to the other. Several Chinese soldiers occupied the other side of the pagoda. They manned an early warning telephone line that ran into Japanese occupied Indochina. The telephone operators in Indochina would notify us of any Japanese air activity.

April 19, 1942
Continued alert duty. Army transports arriving from India with supplies. It is believed that several of the Group in Kunming resigned and went to work for Pan American Ferry Command. Pilots unhappy about the mission types such as strafing and bombing. Loiwing pilots rebel, draw up a letter of resignation. Chennault refuses the letter.

The pilots were grumbling about low level strafing, inductions, resignations, and going back home. Low level strafing was dangerous and something most pilots avoided. The pilots' idea of combat was shooting down enemy aircraft.

"Army transports" C-47 with supplies. The supplies came over the hump from India. "Hump flying" was demanding and dangerous.

April 20, 1942
The 2nd sent Crew Chief's Peeden and Bailey and Armorer Fritzke to help us. Pilots Rossi and Prescott attached to us, returned to the 2nd stationed in Kunming. Pilots Older, Shilling, Dupouy and Groh flew to Namsan, Burma—60 miles north of the Japanese lines.

April 21-22, 1942
Continued alert duty. Pilot Petach and Crew Chief's Blackwell and Woodward returned here after burning Petach's downed aircraft. Clouthier and Quick left by truck for Bhamo, Burma, to purchase food. Rainy season starts.

On April 15 Petach made an emergency landing near the Thai border due to engine problems. Blackwell and Woodward fixed the aircraft, but Petach couldn't take it off because the soil was too sandy. They burned the plane to keep it out of Japanese hands.

April 23, 1942
Continue to bomb and strafe the Japanese. Conditions in the south are serious. Crew Chiefs Cross, Olson, Rogers arrived by truck. Pilot Reed arrived by P-40 from Lashio. Wolf, previously hospitalized, returned to duty. Clouthier and Quick returned from Bhamo, Burma. Pilot Reed arrived after he made an emergency landing at a small remote airfield.

April 24, 1942
The Japanese are near Lashio (250 miles from Kunming) Lashio has been ordered to evacuate the population. The 2nd Pursuit will defend the town until further orders.

A downed Japanese aircraft.

April 25, 1942
Bombed and strafed two long Japanese columns moving up from the South. Three Japanese observation planes were shot down. Pilots Adkins and Bishop arrived from Kunming to support the 3rd.

Tonight we send the trucks to Lashio to get food. We are preparing to evacuate Loiwing. Gen Stilwell (USA) is cornered by the Japanese somewhere in Burma.

April 26, 1942
Orders came to evacuate Loiwing. Destination Mangshi—80 miles by air but longer by road. Japanese are reported near Lashio, Burma. The 2nd Pursuit will stay at Lashio a bit longer then move to Paoshan, China. Swebo, a short distance from Loiwing was bombed. Armorers Poshefko and Wirta inherited auto from folks leaving for Calcutta, India. Hoffman (from Group) flew in from Kunming.

April 27-28, 1942
Evacuation underway. The ground crew stayed at the Hotel. The accommodations were poor. The place is filthy and loaded with malaria. Two of our personnel are already sick.

Mangshi.

Mangshi was cold, filthy, and bug infested. It was better sleeping outside in the truck cab.

April 28, 1942

Weather is rainy and muddy. Loiwing bombed today. The runway was so badly damaged that the 2nd had to send their aircraft here. The Japanese also strafed Lashio. The 3rd Pursuit was sent to intercept the Japanese at Lashio but found none. On the way back they shot down 12 Japanese aircraft. Pilots Smith and Greene crashed. Smith's aircraft a washout, Greene's is fixable. There is a serious shortage of parts.

April 29-30, 1942

Japanese reach Lashio. The Burma escape route to China is cut. No flying, rainy and cloudy weather. Some of the 2nd Pursuit joined us (Pilots Adkins and Donovan). Also 3 RAF men. We have to eat outdoors.

Runway repair. The Chinese human steam rollers.

May 1, 1942

Orders came to evacuate Mangshi. Chennault burned 22 damaged P-40s. All members are to leave for Kunming at their leisure, own expense and best judgment. The pilots will fly, the ground crew will depart by truck or auto.

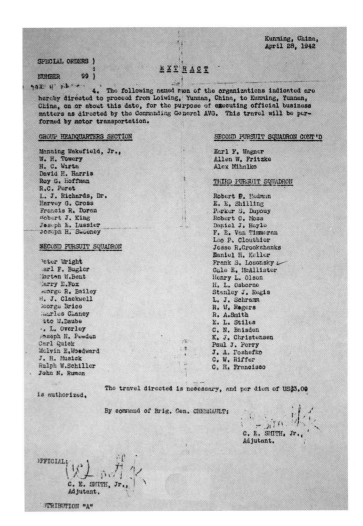

Orders. Note the $3.00 per diem.

May 2, 1942

Pilots Dupouy, Shilling, Hedman, and Foshee plus Radio Men Sweeney and King left for Kunming this morning.

May 3, 1942

Squadron personnel are strung out from here to Kunming. Some will stay overnight at Paoshan or Yunnanyi. Roosevelt sends a message to the AVG urging them to continue until the AAF 23rd Pursuit is able to resume the fight.

Roosevelt's memo to the AVG was posted on the bulletin board. It had little effect on most of us.

"Leaves of absent should be given to the A.V.G. veterans just as soon as replacements have absorbed your experience, training and tradition for rest and recuperation. It is planned that when replacements are adequately trained selected A.V.G. veterans will be recalled to the States or other theaters of operations to impart their combat experience and training to personnel in newly formed units."

"Your President is greatly concerned that the 23rd Group be fully supplied and kept in operation during the critical phase of the operations now pending. He has taken great pride in the world-wide acclaim given the Group and places great hope in its future fighting as rapidly as it is re-equipped."
/s/ Franklin D. Roosevelt

May 4, 1942
Japanese attacked Paoshan, China. Extensive damage. Pilot Foshee killed on the ground by enemy fire. Pilot Bond burnt by enemy action. Pilot Blackburn killed spinning his ship into a lake near Kunming. Japanese reported occupying Wanting, China.

Frank Andersen recalls the Blackburn incident. "I remember Bob Neal called Merlin Kemp and myself up and told us that one of our pilots had gone down in a lake near Kunming. He asked us to get the pilot if we could. A Chinese motor boat took us to the middle of the lake. Took us 3/4 of an hour to get there. The Chinese had marked the crash site with a long flagged bamboo pole. Merlin and I stripped to our shorts and started diving on the wreck. The water was damn cold and visibility—poor. We took turns diving on the aircraft. I could tell it was a P-40 because I could feel the exhaust stacks as we moved our way down to the cockpit. The water was freezing and I could only dive a couple of times before I had to get warmed up. I went down head first and located an open cockpit. I put my hand in the cockpit but couldn't feel a thing.

No parachute straps, no harness, no seat belt. Blackburn had been in the lake for a while and I remember thinking, 'God he's been in the water for two weeks. He's gonna be like putty and that scared me. I'm not going any further—no way.'

On the way back, the motorboat sheered a pin so I yanked a nail out of the boat and made a new one. I told the boatman to be careful taking off but he didn't listen and sheered the nail. We poled the boat back to shore for what seemed to be days. Eventually the Chinese salvaged the aircraft. Blackburn had slid all the way down to the peddles. No one knows why he crashed. He may have been shot up, or had engine trouble, or perhaps mistook the surface of the lake for the landing field. No one knows."

General Wainwritght surrenders Corregidor and the rest of the Philippines to the Japanese.

May 5, 1942
Japanese attacked Paoshan, China. Pilot Foshee buried in Kunming.

May 6, 1942
AVG and Chinese bombing and strafing missions slow the Japanese advance up the Burma Road. The strafing was done with the help of some new P-40s capable of carrying bombs on wing mounts.

May 7-8, 1942
Continued AVG and Chinese strafing and bombing missions at the Salween Gorge. Bartling shot a Japanese observation plane down. Crew Chiefs Olson, Rogers and Armorer Riffer left for Yunnanyi, China.

Downed Japanese aircraft.

The Salween River Gorge Action was recognized as one of the most significant AVG contributions to the war effort. The action slowed the Japanese advance into China.

Battle of the Coral Sea (May 7-8). U.S. Naval aviation is victorious over the Japanese fleet.

May 9, 1942
The AVG and six Chinese Russian bombers bombed and strafed the advancing Japanese columns. Pilot Swartz died in India of injuries received during the 21 March raid on Magwe.

May 10, 1942
Continued bombing and strafing missions. Crew chiefs Olson and Rogers and armorer Riffer return from Yunnanyi, China. McAllister arrived from Yunnanyi after narrowly escaping the advancing Japanese Army. He abandoned his truck, took cover in the hills, eventually found his way to Paoshan.

Gale McAllister's story begins on May 5th. "I was on the Burma Road retreating towards Paoshan when my truck broke down. I was sitting alongside the road when some Chinese picked me up. We drove all night long. Traffic was a mess. Towards dawn as we were getting close to the Salween River bridge the Japanese opened up heavy machine gun fire from behind. We kept moving but the truck had trouble getting around the mountain curves. Occasionally we had to get out and push the truck onto level ground. We were almost at the Salween River bridge when a Chinese General and his bodyguard stopped us. Seems the General wanted us to turn around and fight the oncoming Japanese. I told him the Japanese were just over the top of the hill and I had to get back to my squadron. Eventually he let us go. We didn't go far before we hit another traffic jam. This time I decided not to sit there with the Japanese that close. I started walking towards the bridge which was still a fair distance away. Suddenly Japanese artillery started shooting over my head. The Japanese targets were the on the other side of the river. I gave up on the bridge which I guessed was rigged to explode and headed straight for the river bank. When I got down to the river bank I saw some Chinese soldiers trying to swim

the river. They never made it, they drowned. I figured I didn't want to swim across that much, at least not yet, besides it was still pretty early in the day. I decided to walk upriver, but hadn't taken two steps when the Chinese blew the bridge. I walked upriver most of the day. At dusk I came to a ferry boat where large numbers of Chinese were getting on. The ferry began to sink. The Captain stopped the boarding and threw a number of the passengers off. Eventually we crossed the river but not before nightfall. I was dog tired and cold. A short distance away I stopped at a "commercial" establishment. The proprietor let me sleep on the dirt floor along with lots of other retreating Chinese. The next morning I started out on a mountain trail towards Paoshan. Soon my shoes fell apart. A Chinaman gave me a new pair. I walked all day with a group of Chinese soldiers. That night we arrived at a little village. Some of the Chinese soldiers brought a villager to me. They claimed he was stealing one of their rifles and they wanted me to shoot him. I told them I didn't want to waste my ammunition. Next morning the soldiers and I continued up the trail but soon we parted ways. I walked all night. By morning I was near Paoshan and could make out some P-40s on the airfield. Soon I noticed that they were abandoned P-40s. Wrecks we had left behind in our retreat to Kunming. I came on a Chinese officer who fed me. I felt bad eating his food, but I hadn't eaten anything solid for a couple of days. The officer flagged down a truck and put me on it. Soon I arrived at one of our airfields. Twenty minutes later I was flying back to Kunming in a special C-47 headquarters had sent. My retreat was over and I was home."

A Chinese Army unit on the move.

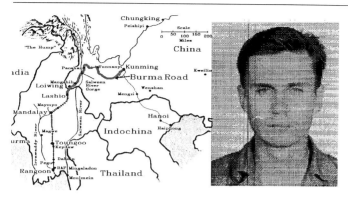

Gale McAllister's Adventure.

Bill Reed.

May 11-12, 1942
Air raid alert. Pilots Laughlin and Donovan and others, of the 1st and 2nd, bombed and strafed Hanoi. Donovan was killed when his ship was hit by anti-aircraft fire and crashed. The other pilots refueled at Mengtsz and returned to Kunming.

May 13-15, 1942
Rainy. The Generalissimo promoted several of pilots in recognition of their flying exploits over Hanoi. The promotions would become effective once vacancies materialized.

May 16, 1942
Our pilots raided Hanoi, damaged a train. Pilot Jones was killed in a practice dive bomb exercise. Chinese intelligence told us to prepare for a major attack on the air field and city.

The Chinese intelligence system was surprisingly effective. It was a network made up of simple telephones, telegraphs, and thousands of Chinese spotters. The spotters reported suspicious activity to feeder stations. The feeder stations in turn, reported it to Chinese Headquarters.

Bill Reed popping his ears.

May 17, 1942
Pilots Smith, Reed, and some pilots of the 2nd strafed Hanoi. Pilot Bishop of the 2nd was shot down and captured near Lao Kay.

May 18-21, 1942
Rainy. Continued alert. General Bissell gave us a pep talk about joining the Army Air Corps at the hostel auditorium. We were also told the 3rd Pursuit would stay in Kunming, the other two squadrons would move to Chungking, China.

The Air Corps made a serious mistake sending Bissell to recruit. His pitch had little effect. He was rude, arrogant, and projected an attitude of indifference towards myself and my comrades. The man turned us off. Most of us felt we'd been shafted and had no desire to serve under his command. The Air Corps would not promise us a 30 day furlough.

May 22, 1942
Pilot Little was killed on a bombing mission. Appears the bomb exploded prematurely while still attached to the aircraft.

May 23-24, 1942
Air raid alert. No action. 10 P-40E aircraft arrived from Karachi, India. Paoshan was bombed.

May 25-27, 1942
Talk of inductions continues, as well as the offers. All members deciding if they are going to accept in-

duction into the Army here or not. They were asked what they wanted if they stayed. Some wanted commissions, others refused all offers.

I remember the 27th well. It was one of the few direct times I talked to General Chennault. He called us in, one at a time. I told the General I wanted to fly. Chennault didn't have a chance to reply. General Bissell spoke up and said "Look the General doesn't have time to give you a recommendation to go to flying school." I replied, "But that's what I want to do. I have flying experience, and I'd like to go to flight school." Bissell replied, "Stay here or else when you get home you will be drafted." I told him I'd take my chances with the draft. It was over in 4 minutes. I would have stayed had they given me flight school, a commission, or the promised thirty day leave.

May 28, 1942
Our armorers were offered commissions if they would stay on as part of the Army Air Corps 23rd Pursuit Group.

As I recall the process was rather selective. Several of our crew chiefs and radio operators were offered commissions. Morgan Vaux recalls, "In the field, we station masters were given re-enlistment offers over the radio by the base operator. I was offered a commission as a First Lieutenant. I rejected the commission because I was suffering from intestinal ailments, was told no leave would be granted and my stay in China was indefinite. On the way home, aboard ship, I was diagnosed by the ship's doctor with hepatitis and spent most of the voyage isolated in sick bay. When I arrived home in September, I was told by the local draft board I had 60 days medical leave before they drafted me."

May 29-30, 1942
Continued alert. Some members of our Group are going to Chungking to take the U.S. Army commissioning exam.

May 31, 1942
Air raid alert at 9:20 AM. Twenty Japanese aircraft bombed Yunnanyi, China. Six Zeros followed the attack and strafed the field.

Yunnanyi was about 120 miles west of Kunming and formerly a training field for Chinese Air Force cadet pilots. The all grass field was now used by the AVG as a forward refueling base for missions into Japanese occupied Burma. Morgan Vaux recalls, "Yunnanyi consisted of a few huts alongside the field. We concealed the fuel drums in the ditches. A distance from the field were two wooden huts, one of which I occupied. My radio station was on a hill in an abandoned pagoda. In one room was my transmitter, receiver and motor generator. In another room was a Stearman trainer without wings or engine."

June 1-2, 1942
Air raid alert. 1st and 2nd scrambled but no action. It was reported 9 Japanese aircraft strafed the airfield at Yunnanyi, China. The Chinese had set up fake bamboo aircraft around the field. Army Air Corps pilots Butsch and Minor were assigned to us. They flew this afternoon and did well. It looks like the Army really intends to take over soon.

What ingenuity. The Chinese built some pretty neat full sized P-40 models out of bamboo. As I recall the Japanese pilots took the bait and shot up the bamboo P-40s much to the relief of Command and the crew chiefs.

June 3, 1942
Six B-25s stationed in Karachi, India bombed Lashio, Burma. Four of the B-25s crashed near Yunnanyi, China. The other two landed here. One of their gunners was killed by an attacking "Zero." One B-17 crashed between Kunming and Chungking.

Frank Andersen recalls that Bissell had ordered six B-25s coming from India to make a detour and bomb Lashio on their way up to Kunming. "As the bombers approached Lashio Japanese fighters jumped them. The Japanese shot two down and sent the others scattering. The survivors went full power to get away but in the process burnt a lot of fuel. As the bombers approached Yunnanyi they ran low on gas. Two crash landed in the mountains. The other two made it to Kunming, one safely, the other dead sticked it in with a dead crew member. What few folks know is that Bissell's adjutant pinned a medal on him for that air strike. Chennault chewed nails but could do little about it. Bissell outranked him."

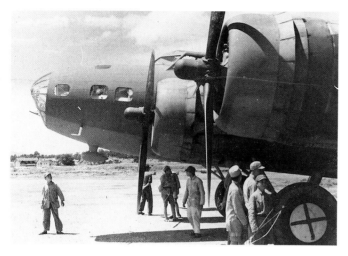

B-17s in Kunming.

A B-25 take off.

Don Rodewald tells a story about the B-25s. "When the 25s came in and wanted bombs, I'd get the coolies to roll them out to the aircraft. We used yo-yo pulls to hoist them into the bomb bay. As soon as we got them loaded some damn pilot or bombardier would change his mind about the load. That left me having to reload the aircraft. I'd secretly "safety" the bombs and with the pilots close by, trigger the bomb release and drop the whole load on the ground. Pilots bolted fast when those bombs hit the ground. Funniest damn sight you ever saw. Coolies calmly rolled the bombs off to the side of the runway and we'd start the load process all over again.

I also remember setting a trap for the Japanese strafers. We piled a bunch of bombs and rocks together at the end of the runway. We fused the bombs and set them to go off. If the Japanese pilots decided to strafe our field they would be in for one hell of a surprise. The Japanese never strafed the field."

June 4, 1942
A Chinese pilot in a Hawk 3 blew up as he was taxiing for takeoff. Apparently his delayed action fuse bomb went off accidentally. Training two new Army pilots in gunnery.

June 5, 1942
Some techs from the 1st and 2nd left for Chungking and Kweilin China. Olson named as Kunming Detachment Commander.

When the Army Air Force came in they set up a normal military complex, a small PX, a commissary, and mess facilities, all of which we were not invited to. I especially missed the ice cream which they ate in front of us.

Kweilin was 300+ miles east of Kunming. The refueling field was used as a jump off point for targets further east. I never went there but Jake Andersen did. Jake recalls, "Kweilin was a pretty important place, a big trade center and also a target for new Japanese bomber pilots. The Japanese had a bombardment school near Hanoi and as a graduation exercise would send the new bomber pilots up to plaster the hell out of the city. The Generalissimo eventually sent the First squadron over to help. After the AVG arrived, I believe it was June 9 or 10, the Japanese sent 18 bombers over and our boys shot 12 of them down. You could hear the brass shell casings (from our P-40s) falling all over the place because we didn't collect the spent casings in collector boxes. Boy did we have a big party after that one. Kweilin was so happy. The town threw a huge party for us. They gave us Scotch, liquors, silk, and bamboo mementos. I remember I went back to the hall after the party and ran into George Burgard, a Philadelphia socialite, a good pilot I guess, but no regular Joe. George was wrapping up a few mementos, so I picked one up myself. Henry Wo helped me decipher the Chinese lettering on the silk. Henry said it was a letter of appreciation from the townsfolk.

Apparently the AVG action was the first resistance anyone had offered since the Japanese invasion. The silk memento was one of the few things I brought home."

The Flying Tiger.

June 6, 1942

Air raid alert. No action. It is believed that spies are notifying the Japanese of our actions. Pilots of the 1st were ordered to fly over the city and pretend they were leaving. If the spy net is active, the Japanese might be lured into attacking Kunming with all three squadrons absent. Our pilots were given more medals for duty at Loiwing and Magwe.

P-40 landings.

If the Japanese had an active spy network in China, we AVGers weren't aware of it.

June 7, 1942
Continued alert. Set a record for damaged aircraft. One pilot overshot the runway and ran his ship into a parked one. Another pilot nosed his P-40 up. Damaged the propeller. A third pilot ground looped. Most of the damage occurred at dusk while landing the aircraft at our auxiliary field—Generalissimo Field. A Chinese pilot had his P-40E landing gear buckle as he was taxiing back to the line.

Battle of Midway (June 4-7). Japanese invasion fleet turned back.

June 8-9, 1942
Continued alert duty. The 1st and 2nd Pursuits continue to leave for Kweilin and Chungking China. Poshefko is ill from some type of stomach disorder. Perry left the hospital. One of the lost B-25 crew members was hospitalized with injuries. They found him near Yunnanyi, China.

June 10, 1942
Our fighters scrambled to intercept Japanese aircraft presumably coming from Lao Kay, Indochina. No action. Two B-25s also took off and circled north of the field—for safety.

June 11, 1942
Continued alert duty. Members of our Squadron are preparing to move to Hostel #2 which is near the field. Heard the Japanese lost a major battle in the Pacific. Midway. The Japanese are now fighting the Chinese for the Costal Provinces presumably to capture Chinese air fields that could be used to bomb Japan. The Squadron has a new mascot, a snow leopard.

As I recall Bob Locke traded a case of condensed milk to some Burmese soldiers for the leopard. The leopard was beautiful, and smart. The dogs would tease her and she'd chase them out to the end of her chain. Sometimes she'd come halfway out and stop, and the dogs would charge her, thinking she was at the end of her chain. She'd spring, catch a dog and

Hostel #2.

Mascot.

flip it. The lucky dogs got away, the others became "leopard meat." Shortly before we disbanded, Bob got PAN AM to fly her home but on a trip up to Kweilin the leopard flipped off the back of a truck and broke her neck. Bob buried her along the road.

June 12-13, 1942
Continued alert duty. The Commanding Officer of the Far East Air Forces arrived from India on a B-24, accompanied by 3 B-25s. Pilots Hedman and Hodges also returned from India with two P-43s. One false air raid warning this afternoon.

June 14, 1942
The Japanese have taken Dutch Harbor in the Aleutian Islands, Alaska.

As I recall, the news came over the Japanese radio. The Japanese successfully invaded and occupied

Attu and Kiska, part of Alaska, United States territory. They did not, however, capture Dutch harbor. At the time, it didn't make much difference to us. We were anxious to go home.

June 15-18, 1942
Routine duties.

June 19, 1942
Chinese pilot crashes.

One of our Chinese pilots landed long and smashed into a village house. He did not survive.

Chinese crash.

June 20, 1942
Chennault and the "Induction Board" left for Kweilin. At Kweilin, no one accepted induction. Chennault telegraphed Stilwell and Brereton on the 23rd and recommended that "inductions" be postponed until October 1st and that they try to get the "contracts" extended.

June 21-22, 1942
Routine duties.

June 23, 1942
Alert flew lead on a 6 ship formation. Haywood, Shilling, and 3 Army boys. The Army boys looked bad.

June 24, 1942
Rained most of the day.

June 25, 1942
Rained today. My flight had the early shift.

June 26, 1942
Went to supply and finance with Hodges to get straightened out before we leave.

June 27, 1942
Crew Chiefs and Armorers got off today. Colonel

Finance records. Did I get paid for July?

Sanders, Army Air Corps, arrived with nine Kittyhawks (P-40Es) after being lost enroute from India.

June 28-29, 1942
Routine duties. Traded my currency in for bonds.

I was sitting on a duffel-bag full of Chinese currency gotten from various enterprises, the sale of my gun, Leica camera, gambling, and other good investments. I took the bag down to the Bank of China in Kunming and exchanged it for a $7,820 bond. As luck would have it the exchange rate was high (The exchange rate varied with the fortunes of battles). When I got to New York I cashed the bond for $7,820. Quite a haul for those days. Thank heavens the U.S. government backed the bonds.

June 30, 1942
Turned Crew Chief operations over to the Air Corps.

June 31, 1942
Some Chinese newsreel cameramen took a bunch of pictures.

July 1-3, 1942
Am getting everything ready for departure. Gave most of my clothes to the houseboys. Most of us felt bad it had to end this way. Col. Haynes, Air Corps activated the U.S. Bomber Command in China.

Frank, and Ernest Bonham.

July 4, 1942
Departed Kunming for Calcutta. The "Flying Tigers" are history.

We sat around the airport for the greater part of the morning saying goodbyes. Finally around 10:30 a number of us boarded a C-47. Within the hour we were out of country, on our way to Calcutta. The trip was uneventful. Since the first action at Kunming December 20, 1941, the "Tigers" had officially shot down 297 Japanese aircraft, blown up equipment, kept the port of Rangoon open for several critical months and stopped the Japanese drive into China proper. Perhaps more important, the "Tigers" were one of the few success stories during those crucial times when little was going right for the Allies. Twenty one "Tigers" had died in China, some close friends.

The "Flying Tigers" cost the U.S. Government $3M for personnel and $8M for aircraft and supplies. $11M total—quite a bargain for the USA.

Who exactly are the "Flying Tigers"? We "original AVGers" believe we have exclusive rights to the name. When the AVG was disbanded on July 4, 1942, so was the name—forever, by Chinese edict from the

Tigers.

Generalissimo Chiang Kai Shek, the Chinese Commander-in-Chief. Others who replaced us also claim the title "Flying Tigers" but those groups were not sponsored by the Chinese people. We "originals" have always faced situations that in some way call into play our "Flying Tiger" association and I'm no exception. Mine came in the 60s when I decked a person who claimed he was an AVGer. He welshed on a $50 bet.

July 5—November 27, 1942
The trip home.

When I left Kunming, Stan and I spent a week in Calcutta, India. We partied every night. On the 13 we left for Delhi, stayed a couple of days, then on to Bombay. We left Bombay for Bangalore then returned to Bombay. We jumped a steamer for Durban, South Africa, and arrived in South Africa on the 14th of August. In Durban we became acquainted with a couple of nice girls, one of whom eventually married Stan. With our visas running out, we left for Bulowayo then on to Port Franeque, South Africa. On the 4 of November, we took a river boat to Leopoldville. We had quite a time getting out of Leopoldville. The Army Air Force gave us no priority on aircraft or ships going back to the States. Meanwhile Stan and I became friendly with the U.S. Vice consul. After waiting a month for transportation, the Vice Consul suggested we become "undesirables." As "undesirables" he had the authority to ship us home. He suggested we throw a "wild" party at one of the grander hotels (The ABC). We proceeded to wreck the place, throwing furniture off the balcony, and generally making ourselves obnoxious. The local authorities promptly kicked us out of South Africa and soon we were on our way home. I arrived in Miami on the 27th of November, 1942. The China war was over for me.

Discharge.

Discharge Certificate.

Chapter V
Postscript–After the "Tigers"

After the AVG disbanded Nancy and I married. I returned to the Far East as a senior mechanic with the China National Aviation Corporation (CNAC), a subsidiary of Pan American. CNAC supplied the Chinese by air from bases in India. I stayed with CNAC until a better job came with Hindustan Aircraft Company. I joined as senior mechanic and built my flight time at the local flying club. Shortly afterwards I returned to the States and built B-24s. With the war in full swing, I reenlisted as an officer cadet and came within two weeks of commissioning when the war ended. I left the AAF and took a civil service job in the Philippines as aircraft maintenance supervisor at Clark Field. On the side I started an import-export business in Manila. A year later I joined Philippines Airlines. I stayed with Philippine Airlines until I joined a venturesome group starting up Trans Asiatic Airlines (TAA). They needed a Chief of Maintenance/pilot. TAA flew the Manila, Hongkong, Bangkok, Rangoon route. It was with TAA that I achieved one of my earliest ambitions, that of a commercial pilot. I left TAA in 1950 and took up farming in Michigan. The farming didn't last and in 1952 I joined Allison Division of General Motors as a senior jet engine service engineer. I spent 30+ years with GM traveling the world as Allison's service representative. I worked with a number of foreign government air forces and also set up repair facilities. When I retired from GM, I joined one of my sons' operations as Executive Officer and Board Member of Part IV, a Columbus, Georgia, restaurant conglomerate.

Through friendships and reunions I've kept in touch with many of the AVG group—all except for my good friend Stanley Regis. Does anyone know his whereabouts?

Stan Regis.

Headquarters American Volunteer Group

THIRD PURSUIT SQUADRON

Kunming, Yunnan, China.
June 23, 1942.

SUBJECT : Recommendation :-

TO   : Whom it may concern :-

I have known Frank S. Losonsky, for a period of ten months, during which time he has been a member of the American Volunteer Group, serving as a crew chief in the Third Pursuit Squadron, 1st A.V.G. I have found him to be diligent, cooperative, and his work very satisfactory. Upon his return to the United States he intends to make application for flight training in the Army Air Corps. Having observed his conduct under fire I am of the opinion that he would make an excellent future combat pilot, and recommend him for flight training.

Robert T. Smith
Robert T. Smith,
Flight Leader, 3rd Pur. Sq.
Assistant Operations Officer,
American Volunteer Group.

R.T. Smith's flight school recommendation.

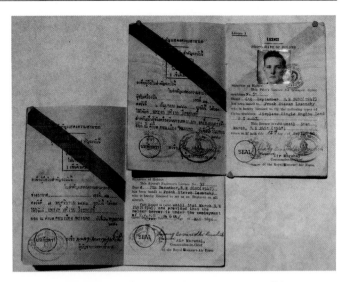

Commercial pilot's license #31—Aircraft engineer's license #32.

HEADQUARTERS FOURTEENTH AIR FORCE
A. P. O. 627, C/O POSTMASTER
NEW YORK CITY, NEW YORK

In reply
refer to: April 1st, 1944.

Mr. Stanley Regis,
Mr. Frank Losonsky,
c/o China National Aviation Corp,
A.P.O. 465

Dear Regis and Losonsky:

Receipt of your letter dated March 28th is acknowledged.

We can always use good crew chiefs over here and I would like very much to have you both in the 14th Air Force. Your knowledge of Chinese methods is invaluable. Unfortunately, I can only induct you both in enlisted grade of Private. However, I can promise you that you will not remain long in that grade, your experience gained while you were with the A.V.G. will most certainly see you through.

I am naturally interested in having any of my old A.V.G. men back and would like to have your decision as soon as possible.

With kindest personal regards, I am,

Most sincerely yours,

C. L. Chennault
C. L. CHENNAULT
Major General, U.S.A.
Commanding.

No comment.

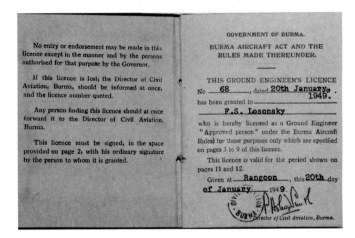

Ground engineer's license #68.

Chapter VI
Photographs

Frank, Theil, and Salasi.

Stan Regis.

Otto Daoge.

Edward Seavey.

Departure.

William Unger.

Eugene McKinney.

William Davis.

Paul Frillman and Ray Hastey.

Jake Anderson.

Van Timmerman.

(L-R): Frank Losonsky, Frank Van Timmer-man, Ernest Bonham, and Carl Quick.

John Young.

Van Timmerman and John Crotty.

Albert Cushing.

John Sommers.

Linstead, Van Timmerman, and Bohnam.

Hodges, Brook, and Olson.

Bill Reed.

Appendices

THE Rangoon Gazette

WEDNESDAY, DECEMBER 24, 1941

RANGOON'S LITTLE "BLITZ"

Rangoon's Air Raid Precautions worked well during the first raid. So did other services, as far as we could see. Just as the official details must be few, so must comment be scanty—and for the same reasons. It is enough to say that, good and not quite so good, nothing that was unexpected happened. The casualties (not officially known at the time of writing) were deeply regrettable. Some day shortly we hope to pay a fitting tribute to the City's first dead by air-raid.

HITLER SACKS HIS GENERALS

Further confirmation that everything is not lovely in the garden for the Germans on the Russian front comes from Berlin itself, where it is officially announced that since Friday Hitler has combined in his hands leadership of the whole armed forces with supreme command of the Army. A few days ago a message from New York quoting a despatch from Kuibishev stated that General von Bock, the Nazi Commander on the Moscow central front, had been relieved of his command. If the Berlin report means anything, Field-Marshal von Brauchitsch, Commander-in-Chief of the armies in Russia, has been made a scapegoat now that the invasion of Russia which in the early weeks held out high hopes of victory to the Germans has turned into a fiasco. Von Brauchitsch and von Bock are outstanding German generals and that they should now be discarded because German plans have gone awry emphasises Hitler's blind desperation to stem the rot.

Before many more days have passed, more German officers will go, the way of these two generals. Field-Marshal Keitel cannot be very happy at the way events are turning out in Russia. This "desk general", one of the few German officers to go through the 1914-18 war without a single citation or promotion, was the father of the plan to invade Russia. Today, as he tags along with Hitler, always at a safe distance from the front, he must be painfully conscious as he sees the Russian adventure crumbling that his chief in due course will turn on him his wrath and rage. At least von Brauchitsch and von Bock, together with the other front generals, were candidly opposed to an attack on Russia and a two-front war. The fate in store for von Rundstedt, whose armies are in retreat in the south, von Leeb, who tried hard but failed to take Leningrad, and Guderian, whose panzer divisions are even now disintegrating into a rabble of mechanised monsters, may be decided shortly. Stark, staring defeat looms up menacingly before Hitler's visions of conquest.

A CORRECT ESTIMATE

It is not usual for the notorious Gayda to write anything that makes sense, but he is right on the mark in his estimate of the ultimate repercussions

HEROISM OF CITY'S CIVIL DEFENCE WORKERS

DUTIES CARRIED OUT WITH CALM AND PRECISION

EFFICIENT WORK BY HOSPITAL STAFFS

By a Staff Reporter

THE quiet heroism of Rangoon's Civil Defence workers created an indelible impression on my mind as I moved about Rangoon at the hour of its first air raid yesterday morning. In the past they have been the butt of ill-timed humour; yesterday those who laughed were the ones who turned to them for succour.

While the raid was still in progress, while the bombs were still falling, the women who manned the ambulances drove their vehicles regardless of personal danger to carry the wounded to the hospitals and emergency dressing stations. And they drove in cool, efficient, self-possessed manner, attending to their duties with admirable calm.

I saw A.R.P. workers and members of the auxiliary fire services running into burning buildings and others damaged but still standing, rescuing the injured and carrying out the dead. Overhead there was the rat-a-tat of machine-guns; about them bombs exploded.

I also saw doctors and nurses in the Rangoon General Hospital and the six emergency hospitals living up to the highest traditions of their profession. The hospitals were busy dealing with wounded men, women and children, and I was impressed by the cool precision with which the doctors and nurses attended to the cases before despatching them to the wards set aside for their particular type of injuries. The operating theatres worked at top speed as the small army of surgeons sought to save the lives of those to whom Death had been dealt out.

The fatalities suffered by Rangoon are not yet known. But whatever they are they would certainly have been higher but for those whose lives have been dedicated to the alleviation of human suffering.

U Tharrawaddy Maung Maung, Minister of Health and Public Works, made a tour of hospitals in Rangoon yesterday. He first visited the emergency hospital at St. Philomena's Convent, Prome Road, and then went on to the Dufferin Hospital from where he proceeded to the Myoma National Boys' High School.

While he was there the air raid alarm was sounded but U Tharrawaddy Maung Maung completed his inspection and went to the General Hospital soon after his arrival there which was bombed.

The confusion which ensued at the hospital was for the most part, in his opinion, due to the fact that pedestrians rushed into the building for shelter. Steps, he said, should be taken to prevent a repetition of this.

He added that doctors, nurses, students and helpers rallied splendidly when the casualties began to arrive and he was favourably impressed with the efficient way in which they carried out their duties. We understand that the Hon. Minister himself helped when the casualties arrived.

U Tharrawaddy Maung Maung said that if the staffs of other hospitals in the city could work as smoothly in a similar emergency, as he had no doubt they could, the prompt and effective treatment of air raid victims was assured.

NEW BURMA RAILWAY TIMINGS

A Burma Railways notice says: In connection with the change of time to take place at 2-0 hours (Burma Standard Time) on the morning of 24th instant, the following trains will leave Rangoon on the 23rd instant one hour earlier than the time-table timings, to enable them to arrive at destinations and

RANGOON'S FIRST "BAPTISM OF FIRE"

MORNING RAID BY JAPANESE BOMBERS AND FIGHTERS

BRILLIANT WORK BY OUR FIGHTER AIRCRAFT

DESTRUCTION OF NINE BOMBERS AND ONE FIGHTER CONFIRMED

FIRES QUICKLY UNDER CONTROL BY LOCAL FIRE SERVICES

GOOD WORK BY A.-A. CREWS IN DOCK AREA AND AT MINGALADON

An R.A.F. communique issued from Army Headquarters, Rangoon, at 7 p.m. yesterday (Tuesday) states:

An air raid warning was sounded at approximately 10-10 hours today when information was received that three waves of approximately 50 to 60 Japanese bombers escorted by fighters were approaching Rangoon from south and east.

British and American fighters despatched to intercept caught the raiders just before they reached the city. When attacked by the interceptors the raiders broke formation. A number of bombers, however, reached their objectives, which appeared to be Mingaladon and the docks.

Slight damage was sustained at the former, including a block of buildings and a small quantity of fuel destroyed. The R.A.F. sustained some casualties to their ground staff.

Brilliant work of the fighters resulted in the destruction of nine bombers and one fighter confirmed, with several so damaged that they are unlikely to have reached their base.

On the enemy's return flight they were again attacked by our fighters and further losses were inflicted.

Three fighter aircraft were lost as a result of the engagement, but one of the pilots who escaped by parachute and was machine-gunned by the enemy is safe. The second pilot is still missing.

Local A.-A. crews went into action for the first time in the dock area and at Mingaladon and did well in their first "baptism of fire".

A patrol of our troops became engaged with enemy forces at Messiar. They succeeded in shooting them up and withdrew without casualties.

A communique issued by the Department of the Commissioner of Civil Defence at 10 p.m. last night states that Rangoon had an air raid warning shortly after 10 a.m. The enemy air raiders approached the city in two waves and a number of bombs were dropped. Some damage was caused, but casualties were fairly heavy almost all of which were caught in the open.

ENEMY PLANE SHOT DOWN BY A.-A. FIRE

RANGOON RECEIVED ITS first "baptism of fire" yesterday morning when Japanese planes appeared out of a clear December sky to bomb and machine-gun the city. The alert sounded shortly after the city had commenced its business life and the majority of the population was out-of-doors.

Feeling perhaps that the alert would be similar to the one of two Saturdays ago, when enemy planes came over Rangoon but did not drop bombs, people did not seek immediate shelter. Instead they stood at street corners watching the planes as they circled overhead.

The first indication that it was the

known of casualties among those who took cover.

The raid itself did not last very long, but the all-clear was not sounded until four and a-half hours later. Several of the enemy's planes were brought down, crashing in various parts of the city.

VISIT TO DESERT BATTLE ZONE

BEHAVIOUR OF GERMAN AND ITALIAN PRISONERS

Cairo: A Frenchwoman named Mlle Curie told a "Mirror" reporter how she recently paid a visit to the Western Desert. The first woman allowed to penetrate so far into the battle zone, she recounts her meetings with British and Imperial soldiers and the pride with which she made the acquaintance of veterans from several fronts. Moreover "suddenly across the sand came two big cars loaded with German and Italian

Rangoon Paper

Headquarters American Volunteer Group

THIRD PURSUIT SQUADRON

Kunming, Yunnan, China.
June 23, 1942.

SUBJECT : Recommendation :-

TO   : Whom it may concern :-

I have known Frank S. Losonsky, for a period of ten months, during which time he has been a member of the American Volunteer Group, serving as a crew chief in the Third Pursuit Squadron, 1st A.V.G. I have found him to be diligent, cooperative, and his work very satisfactory. Upon his return to the United States he intends to make application for flight training in the Army Air Corps. Having observed his conduct under fire I am of the opinion that he would make an excellent future combat pilot, and recommend him for flight training.

Robert T. Smith
Robert T. Smith,
Flight Leader, 3rd Pur. Sq.
Assistant Operations Officer,
American Volunteer Group.

Mitsubishi A6M-1/2/-2N ZERO-SEN
in Japanese Naval Air Service

Richard M. Bueschel

Size: 8 1/2" x 11" over 150 photographs
64 pages, soft cover
ISBN: 0-88740-754-4 $14.95

NAKAJIMA Ki-43 HAYABUSA
in Japanese Army Air Force
RTAF-CAF-IPSF Service

Richard M. Bueschel

Size: 8 1/2" x 11" over 100 b/w photographs
64 pages, soft cover
ISBN: 0-88740-804-4 $14.95

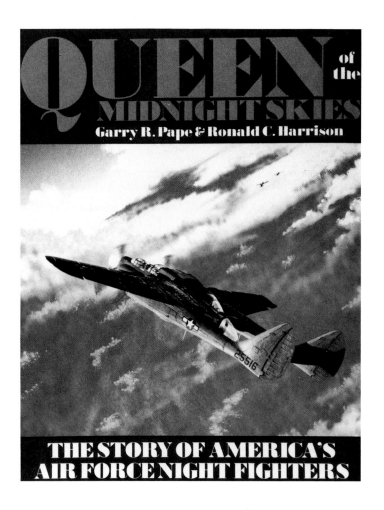

QUEEN OF THE MIDNIGHT SKIES
The Story of America's USAF Night Fighters

Garry R. pape & Ronald C. Harrison

Size: 8 1/2" x 11"   over 700 photographs, maps, squadron victory listing
368 pages, hard cover
ISBN: 0-88740-415-4 $45.00

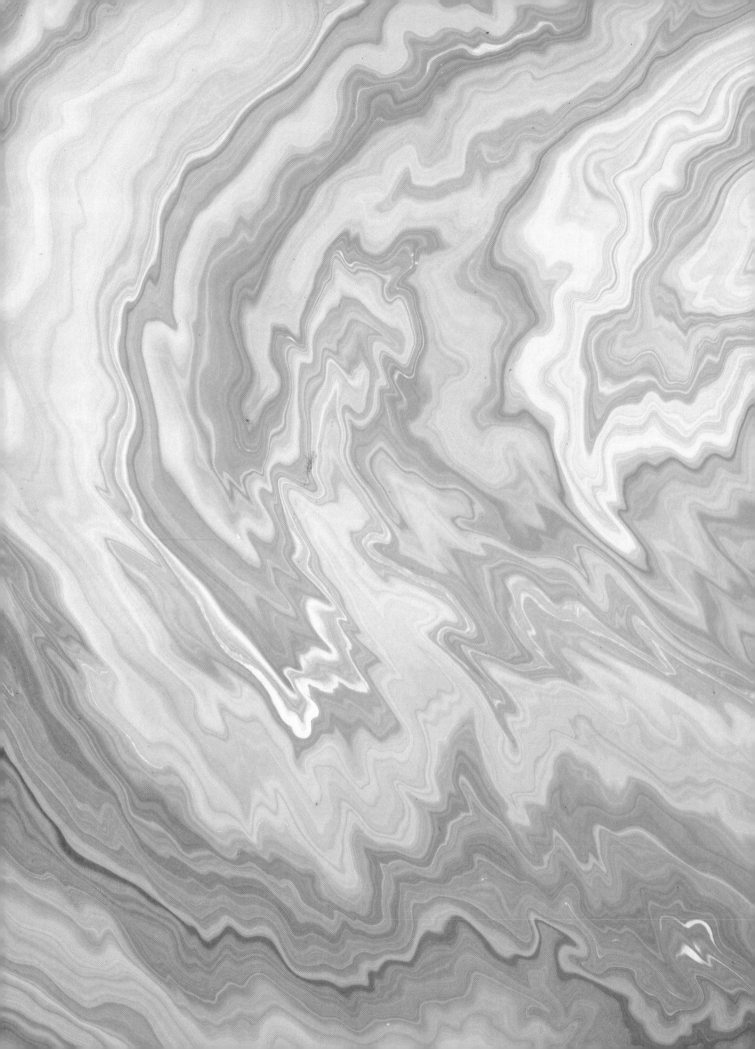